Understanding the European Constitution

Werner Weidenfeld

Understanding the European Constitution

With the collaboration of:
Janis A. Emmanouilidis,
Almut Möller and Sibylle Reiter

| **Verlag** Bertelsmann**Stiftung**

Bibliographic information published by Die Deutsche Nationalbibliothek

Die Deutsche Nationalbibliothek lists this publication in the Deutsche Nationalbibliografie; detailed bibliographic information is available online at http://dnb.d-nb.de.

Responsible: Janis A. Emmanouilidis, Almut Möller, Dr. Dominik Hierlemann
Language editor: Rob Blackhurst, London
Translation: Alfred Clayton, Hamburg
Editing: Barbara Serfozo, Berlin
Diagrams and tables: Lothar Kreutzer, Les Shrags, Entraching

Production editor: Sabine Reimann
Cover design: Nadine Humann
Cover photo: © picture-alliance/dpa/dpaweb
Typesetting and print: Hans Kock Buch- und Offsetdruck GmbH, Bielefeld
ISBN 978-3-89204-932-6

www.bertelsmann-stiftung.de/publications

Contents

Diagrams and tables

Abbreviations

C·A·P	Center for Applied Policy Research
CFSP	Common Foreign and Security Policy
EAC	European Atomic Energy Community
EEAS	European External Action Service
EC	European Communities
ECSC	European Coal and Steel Community
EDA	European Defence Agency
EDC	European Defence Community
EEC	European Economic Community
EFTA	European Free Trade Area
EMS	European Monetary System
EMU	Economic and Monetary Union
EP	European Parliament
EPC	European Political Community
EPC	European Political Cooperation
EPP	European People's Party
ESDP	European Security and Defence Policy
EU	European Union
Euratom	European Atomic Energy Community
Europol	European Police Force
JHA	Cooperation on Justice and Home Affairs
SEA	Single European Act
TCE	Treaty establishing a Constitution for Europe
UN	United Nations
VAT	Value Added Tax

Preface

After the disastrous experiences of two world wars, it seems almost miraculous that the states of the European Union (EU) now live in peace, freedom and prosperity. On May 1, 2004, in the largest round of enlargement in its history, the EU welcomed ten new members and then two more on January 1, 2007, finally putting an end to the Cold War division of Europe. After the fall of the Berlin Wall, the dissolution of the Soviet Union, and the transformation to democracy and market economy, its 27 member states cherish common goals and values.

Political decision-makers and EU experts agree that the existing EU Treaties are no longer transparent and efficient enough to govern a Union of 27 and eventually even more member states. The European Union requires a reform of its Treaties.

On October 29, 2004, the Heads of State and Government signed the "Treaty establishing a Constitution for Europe" at a ceremony in Rome. The Constitution combines all previous Treaties in one single text. Its primary innovations include the reform of institutions and decision-making procedures, the inclusion of fundamental rights such as freedom of thought, the equality of men and women, the rejection of capital punishment, and the enhancement of the role of the European Parliament.

But the Treaty establishing a Constitution for Europe still has to be ratified by each of the 27 member states before it can take effect. As of February 2007, only 18 countries had adopted the Treaty even though the ratification process was supposed to have been completed by the end of 2006. Taken together, the 18 ratifications amount to more than 50 percent of the population of all the EU countries. Nevertheless, the "non" of the French and the "nee" of the Dutch, coupled with the postponement of the referenda in the United Kingdom and other countries, has plunged the EU into crisis.

Though the referenda defeats were a setback, the picture may not be as bleak for the European Union as is often claimed. Unsuccessful referenda in France and the Netherlands could rouse Europe out of its apathy. In June 2005, the EU embarked on a year-long "period of reflection" in the ratification process to discuss the actual contents of the Constitution with the European electorate. Far too many people still see the EU as a complicated, opaque and remote organization in Brussels. It is imperative that the EU brings its policies closer to its citizens and demonstrates that the core elements of the present Constitutional Treaty will improve the lives of Europe's citizens by making the EU more democratic and transparent.

Despite a whole series of positive features, the European Constitutional Treaty has been fundamentally flawed from the beginning. It is long, complicated and incomprehensible to average readers. This became painfully apparent in France where hardly anyone read the 480-page document, despite the fact that the Constitution was mailed directly to 42 million voters. Many simply relied upon the views of the Constitution's critics.

This guide is designed to help ordinary citizens understand the Constitution. The origins, drafting and structure of the Constitution are explained along with the most important EU institutions and their functions. What changes will the Constitutional Treaty make? And how will it affect EU decisions in the future? This book answers these questions.

The Constitution is a decisive step in the right direction when compared to the earlier Treaties: it makes the EU more democratic and gives it the power to act.

But the EU faces growing apathy among its electorate, which threatens the European project. Member states have so far failed to familiarize citizens with both the Constitution and the workings of the European Union. Clearly, doing so would constitute an Olympian feat well worth the effort. Despite recent set backs, when we look back on 50 years of integration, we see that the process of European unification, notwithstanding the occasional disagreements, has always been guided by a political vision to which there is no alternative: peace, freedom, prosperity and a shared belief in democracy, pluralism, tolerance and fellowship.

I would like to thank everybody who contributed to the success of this book: Janis A. Emmanouilidis, Almut Möller and Sibylle Reiter for providing substantial input, Dominik Hierlemann for the coordination of the project and Rob Blackhurst for his careful work as a language editor.

Prof. Dr. Dr. h.c. Werner Weidenfeld
Member of the Board of the Bertelsmann Stiftung, Guetersloh
Director of the Center for Applied Policy Research (C·A·P),
Ludwig-Maximilians-University, Munich

1 Why does the EU need a fundamental reform of its treaties?

"We should not forget that 65 percent of Europeans believe that the Union needs a constitution. Then, in the eyes of the world, will Europe truly begin to exist."

Valéry Giscard d'Estaing, former French President and President of the European Convention.

For many years, EU citizens were given the impression that European integration was primarily an economic project. Yet, the Union is far more than this. In many respects it possesses the qualities of a state. However, even for experts, its policies, institutions and decision-making procedures can be difficult to understand.

Goal: more transparency

The Union had never had a single fundamental legal document. The total body of EU law, known as the *acquis communautaire*, is based on a number of different treaties, which are very difficult to read and comprehend. Conflating the European Treaties in a single text would, it was hoped, lead to greater transparency.

Goal: improved decision-making

Another goal of the Constitution was to improve the EU's institutional setting and to streamline decision-making procedures within the Union in order to improve its overall functioning. In the previous rounds of reform in the 1980s and 1990s—the Single European Act, and the Treaties of Maastricht, Amsterdam and Nice—there were repeated attempts to do so, but it proved impossible to achieve a resounding breakthrough.

> "CONVINCED that, while remaining proud of their own national identities and history, the peoples of Europe are determined to transcend their former divisions and, united ever more closely, to forge a common destiny,
>
> CONVINCED that, thus 'united in diversity', Europe offers them the best chance of pursuing ... the great venture which makes of it a special area of human hope ..."
>
> *Extract from the Preamble to the Treaty establishing a Constitution for Europe*

Goal: more democracy

A third goal of the constitutional process was to make European politics more democratic. Despite the fact that it has acquired considerable powers in recent decades, the only directly elected EU institution—the European Parliament (EP)—is still not as powerful a legislative chamber as the Council of Ministers, made up of representatives of the governments of member states.

National parliaments have little opportunity to voice their views on European policies that have a major influence on the states they govern. And it is undeniable that the European legislative process deprives them of some powers. With the exception of the elections to the European Parliament, the European electorate still cannot make its views known directly, for example, through a citizens' initiative. Though it is the Union's duty to respect the basic rights of EU citizens, its Treaties do not contain a list of guaranteed fundamental rights.

Securing long-term ability to make decisions

A substantial reform of the existing Treaties became imperative due to the accession of ten new member states on May 1, 2004. At the stroke of midnight, the Union grew from 15 to 25 member states—a serious challenge to the EU's ability to function. On January 1, 2007 Bulgaria and Romania also joined the European Union. Each of the 27 countries is represented in the institutions, takes part in the voting, and vigorously promotes its various interests. It was obvious that the EU bodies and institutions could not simply grow in line with the increase in the number of member states without placing a massive strain on the enlarged Union. The time was ripe for reforms that would ensure the functioning of an EU of 27 and eventually more member states.

Treaty, Constitution, or both?

EU citizens often voice anxieties that the Constitutional Treaty will emasculate (or even replace) the constitutions of the European nation-states. Since the EU is not a state, but a confederation, (that is, a free union of sovereign states) this will not happen, whether or not the Constitution is adopted.

A constitution determines the fundamental structure of a state. Constitutional scholars will argue that it enshrines the basic rights of citizens, explains the values which the state cherishes, and describes how the state's institutions function. It dictates the division of powers between the executive, the legislative and the judiciary, and the instruments that are available to implement policy.

All these elements are present in the European Constitutional Treaty, which refers to certain values (see Article I-2), specifies the rights of EU citizens in the Charter of Fundamental Rights (Articles II-61 to II-114), and describes how the European Union's institutions operate (European Parliament, Council of Ministers, European Commission, European Court of Justice, etc.).

However, the European Constitution, by its very nature, is an international treaty which the member states have concluded among themselves. Before it can go into effect, it must be ratified by all member states.

The European Constitution does not establish a European state; it merely defines the framework within which the European Union can act. Whereas it is true that the Constitution and the legislation passed by EU institutions have priority over the laws of the member states, they complement rather than replace the national constitutional arrangements. In each member state domestic law will continue to apply to matters legislated on by Parliament, and the European Constitutional Treaty will apply in dealings with the European Union.

Setback for the Constitution

In spring 2005, the French and Dutch rejection of the Constitutional Treaty in two separate popular votes, and the subsequent suspension of the referenda in the United Kingdom and other countries shortly afterwards were a severe blow to the Constitution's ratification process. The impact was felt all the more keenly since France and the Netherlands were founding members of the European Union.

In light of the failed referenda, the Heads of State and Government at the Brussels summit in June 2005 gave themselves a 12-months period of reflection, and agreed to conduct a public debate about the Constitution.

However, the "no" votes do not necessarily mean that the EU is terminally unpopular: saying "no" to the Constitution is not the same as saying "no" to Europe. In the final analysis, 83 percent of the French and 78 percent of the Dutch are in favor of their country being a member of the European Union. Research showed that 31 percent of the French rejected the Constitution because they were afraid that it would lead to a deterioration in the employment situation. And 32 percent of the Dutch said they had voted "nee" because they had not been properly informed about its contents.

This lack of information about the contents of the Constitution meant that it attracted contradictory criticism from across the political spectrum. For some, it was a neoliberal document that would destroy Europe's social protections. For others, it became a federalist manifesto that would accelerate the drive towards a "United States of Europe." In defeat, there was similar confusion—had the French and Dutch rejected an "ever closer union" and stood up for their national independence? Or had they simply been expressing their discontent with globalization and unfettered free markets?

A wide variety of reasons have been given for the French and Dutch referendum defeat. Pro-Constitution campaigners were accused of overstating their case implying that defeat would somehow result in Europe's slide back into war. The prospect of further enlargement, particularly of Turkey joining the EU, was a major factor in France and the Netherlands.

In both countries, the "no" camps were emboldened by a powerful anti-establishment mood. France's leading figures calling for a "yes" vote, including President Jacques Chirac, were deeply unpopular. In the Netherlands, "no" campaigners powerfully pointed out that the same elite who were calling for a "yes" vote had signed up to the euro and encouraged mass migration—two policies that were profoundly unpopular at the time of the vote. Localized national gripes with the EU also played a part. The Dutch electorate were angry that, per head, they were the biggest contributors to the EU budget.

In response to these referendum results, the EU has devised an information strategy designed to familiarize the European electorate with the text of the Constitution. The intention is to involve EU citizens, civil society actors, social partners, parliaments and political parties in a wide debate. On October 13, 2005, the European Commission unveiled *Plan D* (*Democracy, Dialogue and Debate*)—designed to keep the constitutional process on the rails, and to rekindle the electorate's confidence in the European Union.

Citizens must be involved

When the Constitution was being drawn up, European politicians decided to allow EU citizens to take an active part in the discussions surrounding the genesis of the constitutional text. However, many people felt that they had been ignored. This was a serious mistake that should not be repeated. The involvement of EU citizens will succeed only if an attempt is made to elucidate the principal features of the Constitutional Treaty, without bombarding voters with an impenetrable thicket of rules and regulations.

"Being a member of a family should not prevent you from continuing to be an individual. Being a member of the European Union should not prevent you from continuing to be a citizen of your own country."

Valéry Giscard d'Estaing

What kind of Europe does the electorate actually want?

Support for the European project depends on EU citizens understanding the workings of the European Union. The electorate wants to know which policies and laws are formulated on the European level. Thus, the EU must present its political program in the same way as national governments. Citizens want to know who is responsible for which decisions in economic policy, foreign and security policy, and in the fight against international terrorism and crime. For many years, the Eurobarometer polls have shown that EU citizens want a Europe that provides them with peace, security, prosperity and social justice. They need the tools to be able to judge whether the EU has addressed these issues effectively.

So far, the EU's efforts to attract the attentions of Europe's citizens have not been a great success. On the one hand, there is a need for a structured information policy. On the other, EU institutions must be adapted to enable them to deal with enlargement.

2 The history of the European Union

The entry into force of a European Constitution would constitute a climax in the process of European integration as the new basic document brings together half a century of its history.

Europe in ruins after World War II

Europe after the Second World War was characterized by the decline of the European states and the formation of two power blocs in east and west. The populations of European states suffered gravely in the aftermath of war. Refugees and deportees, hunger and widespread destruction were rife.

The new world powers, the United States and the Soviet Union had far greater resources than those of the comparatively small European nation-states. Western European states hoped, on the one hand, to achieve peace and prosperity by means of a political union, and, by acting together, to recover some of the influence they had individually lost. At the same time, following the experience of Nazi Germany, there was a desire to prevent European states becoming aggressive.

Churchill's vision of the "United States of Europe"

As early as September 19, 1946, then British Prime Minister, Winston Churchill, spoke in Zurich of his vision of the "United States of Europe." All those European states, which were willing to participate—though at the time he excluded the United Kingdom—were to join together under the leadership of France and Germany. Against the background of the deteriorating Cold War, the (west) European movement that now began to emerge received growing support (see table, pp. 20–22).

"Our constant aim must be to build and fortify the strength of the United Nations organization. Under and within that world concept we must re-create the European family in a regional structure called—it may be—the United States of Europe."

Winston Churchill, Speech at the University of Zurich, September 19, 1946

Founding members of the ECSC/EEC: Belgium, France, Germany, Italy, Luxembourg, the Netherlands

The European integration project actually began on April 18, 1951 with the decision to establish the European Coal and Steel Community (ECSC), also known as the "Schuman Plan." The ECSC originated in a proposal by Robert Schuman, the French Foreign Minister, and the French Commissioner for Planning Jean Monnet. Six states—Belgium, Germany, France, Italy, Luxembourg and the Netherlands—were signatories to this document, which was designed to put an end to the hereditary enmity between France and Germany. It was hoped that this economic integration would eventually lead to political union.

First economic integration, then political union

However, the path of European unification was far from smooth. Its progress was always accompanied by unforeseen triumphs and disasters. On May 27, 1952 the Treaty establishing a European Defence Community (EDC) was signed and in September 1952 the six participating countries decided to devise a constitution for a European Political Community (EPC). The plan was to integrate the ECSC and the EDC into the EPC.

However, in August 1954, the European Defence Community was rejected by the French National Assembly. This put an end to the first attempt to draw up a European constitution and to establish a European Political Community. However, the constitutional process clearly had its antecedents at this brave attempt 50 years earlier.

The history of the European

9 May 1950	Robert Schuman, the French Minister of Foreign Affairs, proposes the establishment of the European Coal and Steel Community (ECSC).
18 April 1951	Treaty establishing the ECSC (Treaty of Paris) signed by Belgium, Germany, France, Italy, Luxembourg and the Netherlands (the "Six").
27 May 1952	Treaty establishing the European Defence Community (EDC) is signed, but it is rejected in 1954 by the French National Assembly.
25 March 1957	The "Six" sign the "Treaties of Rome" establishing the European Economic Community (EEC) and the European Atomic Energy Community (EAC).
1 July 1968	Customs union comes into force and common external tariff is introduced.
1 January 1973	Three new members join the EC: Denmark, the United Kingdom and Ireland.
7–10 June 1979	The first direct and general elections for the European Parliament (EP) are held in the nine EC member states.
1 January 1981	Greece becomes the tenth member of the EC.
14 June 1985	The EC Commission publishes the White Paper on completing the internal market.
2–3 December 1985	The member states adopt the "Single European Act" (SEA), which reforms the institutional system, extends the responsibilities of the Community and provides a legal framework for co-operation in foreign affairs.
1 January 1986	After the accession of Portugal and Spain, the EC has twelve members.
1 July 1987	The Single European Act (SEA), which modifies the Treaties of Rome, comes into force.
26–27 June 1989	The heads of state and government adopt the Delors plan for the creation of an Economic and Monetary Union (EMU) in three stages.

Community/European Union

The heads of state and government adopt the "Treaty of Maastricht" establishing the European Union, which comprises three pillars: the European Communities (EEC, ECSC, EAC), the Common Foreign and Security Policy (CFSP), and Cooperation on Justice and Home Affairs (JHA).	**9–10 December 1991**
The Treaty of Maastricht comes into force.	**1 November 1993**
Finland, Austria and Sweden join the EU, which now comprises 15 members.	**1 January 1995**
The Schengen Agreement comes into force. Border controls between the Benelux countries, France, Germany, Portugal and Spain disappear.	**26 March 1995**
Denmark, Finland, Sweden and non-EU countries Iceland and Norway join the Schengen Agreement.	**19 December 1996**
The heads of state and government adopt the Treaty of Amsterdam which reforms the Treaty of Maastricht.	**16–17 June 1997**
Italy adopts the Schengen Agreement.	**26 October 1997**
Austria adopts the Schengen Agreement.	**1 December 1997**
The EMU begins in eleven Member States (Austria, Belgium, Finland, France, Germany, Ireland, Italy, Luxembourg, the Netherlands, Portugal and Spain).	**1 January 1999**
The Treaty of Amsterdam comes into force.	**1 May 1999**
The Charter of Fundamental Rights of the European Union, which was drawn up by a convention headed by former German President Roman Herzog, is solemnly proclaimed.	**7 December 2000**
The heads of state and government adopt the Treaty of Nice, the institutional reforms of which are designed to prepare the EU for the next enlargement.	**7–11 December 2000**
Greece becomes the twelfth member of the Eurozone.	**1 January 2001**

1 January 2002	The Euro becomes the legal tender in the twelve countries of the Eurozone.
28 February 2002	First meeting of the Convention on the Future of the EU, which draws up a draft Constitution together with the accession candidates.
1 February 2003	The Treaty of Nice comes into force.
18 July 2003	Valéry Giscard d'Estaing, the President of the Convention, presents the Convention's draft proposals for a Treaty establishing a Constitution for Europe to the Italian Presidency of the Council.
4 October 2003	Start of the Intergovernmental Conference on the Convention's draft Constitution, at which the governments have to decide whether to accept or reject the proposals.
12–13 December 2003	The first attempt to conclude the Intergovernmental Conference on the Convention's draft Constitution is a failure.
1 May 2004	Ten new Member States – Cyprus, the Czech Republic, Estonia, Hungary, Latvia, Lithuania, Malta, Poland, Slovakia and Slovenia – join the EU, which now has 25 members.
17–18 June 2004	On their second attempt the heads of state and government under the Irish Presidency adopt the "Treaty establishing a Constitution for Europe".
29 October 2004	The "Treaty establishing a Constitution for Europe" is signed at a solemn ceremony on the Capitol Hill in Rome by the 25 EU heads of state and government. Ratification by the national parliaments begins.
29 May 2005	The French referendum on the Constitution fails.
1 June 2005	The Dutch referendum on the Constitution fails.
3 October 2005	Start of accession negotiations with Croatia and Turkey.
1 January 2007	Bulgaria and Romania join the EU. Slovenia joins the Eurozone.

Source: Werner Weidenfeld / Wolfgang Wessels:
Europa von A bis Z, Taschenbuch der europäischen Integration, Baden-Baden 2005

"Europe will not be made all at once, or according to a single plan. It will be built through concrete achievements which first create a de facto solidarity."

Robert Schuman, Basic declaration on the ECSC,
Paris, May 9, 1950

2.1 The Treaties of Rome and northern enlargement

The ECSC foreign ministers meeting in Messina, Italy at the beginning of June 1955 led to the "Treaties of Rome," which marked the foundation of the European Economic Community (EEC) and the European Atomic Energy Community (Euratom).

The aims of the EEC included a customs union designed to dismantle trade barriers, and the introduction of a common external tariff. Euratom was designed to promote the development of the nuclear industry in the six member states.

The three Treaties relating to the ECSC, the EEC and Euratom were combined on April 8, 1965 in order to lay the foundations of the European Communities (EC). This Treaty came into effect on July 1, 1967.

EC's northern enlargement in 1973: the United Kingdom, Ireland and Denmark

Another landmark in the history of the European Union was the summit in The Hague in December 1969, which reached agreement on the northern enlargement of the European Community. Accession negotiations with the United Kingdom, Ireland, Denmark and Norway were concluded in January 1972. The ensuing referenda led to majorities in favor of accession in every country except Norway, which has remained outside of the EU ever since.

By the beginning of 1973, the EC had become a nine-member strong club. In order to coordinate their foreign policies, the EC foreign ministers also reached an agreement in October 1970 on the so-called "European Political Cooperation."

Establishing the European Council

The implementation of the goals laid down in the Treaty of Rome required the establishment of new or the reform of already existing institutions, the development of a common economic

Signing the Treaties of Rome in the Palazzo dei Conservatori on the Capitol Hill on March 25, 1957. The EU Constitution was also signed here on October 29, 2004.

and monetary policy, and a new financial system. The European Council was established in 1974. It brought together the Heads of State and Government of the member states, who now met at least twice a year in order to determine the guidelines of EC policy.

As a result of the European Monetary System (EMS) established in 1979, the goal of economic and monetary union gradually came within reach. But despite such individual progress, there continued to be a great deal of uncertainty about how to complete European integration. For this reason, the then Belgian Prime Minister Leo Tindemans was commissioned in 1974 to formulate a plan for transforming the EC into a "European Union."

Tindemans Report

In his report, Tindemans called for the creation of a single central decision-making institution, the strengthening of the common foreign policy, and a gradual deepening of European integration. But at the time the EC countries were not able to follow through these recommendations with a concrete program to establish a European Union.

By the end of the 1970s, much had been achieved: the free movement of goods, common external tariffs, the common foreign trade policy and the "communitarization" of important

After signing the Treaty establishing a Constitution for Europe

areas, which contributed to the prosperity and democratic stability of western Europe. However, the single market was still not particularly effective; restrictions on the freedom of movement continued. With no sign of a real breakthrough towards economic and monetary union, political union seemed beyond reach.

2.2 Pressure for reform in the 1980s and southern enlargement

From the middle of the 1970s, as the global economic climate worsened, the economy of the EC entered a state of crisis. Frictions arose between community interests at the EC level, and the concerns of individual member states, exposing the weakness of the European institutions.

Crisis in the 1970s: Eurosclerosis

As the European Commission developed into an administrative center, the work of the central decision-making institution, the Council of Ministers, was increasingly seen as ineffective and inscrutable. At the same time, the EC had reached its financial limits. Two-thirds of its expenditure was devoted to agriculture while other areas were simply neglected. This overall malaise became known as "eurosclerosis." It seemed to observers that the European ideal had lost its momentum.

Members of the European Union 1957 to 2004

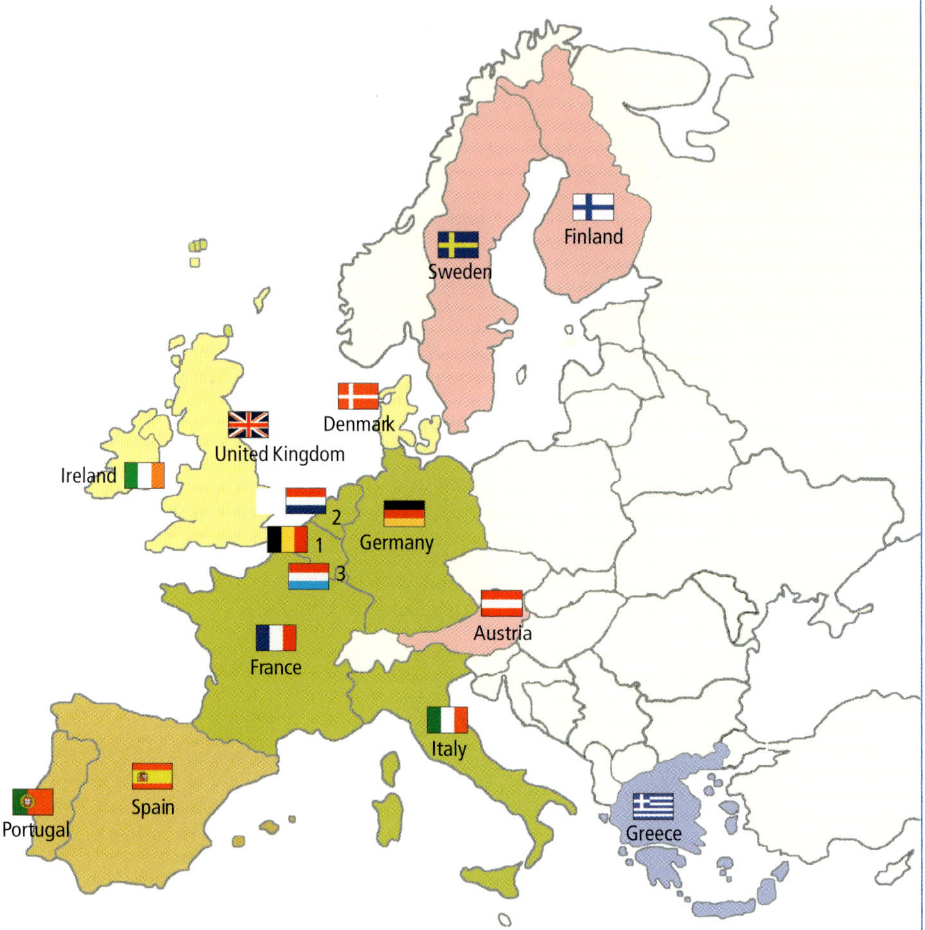

1957 (6 members) Benelux countries: Belgium (1), Netherlands (2), Luxembourg (3); France, Germany and Itlay

1973 (9 members) Accession of Denmark, Ireland and United Kingdom

1981 (10 members) Accession of Greece

1986 (12 members) Accession of Portugal and Spain

1995 (15 members) Accession of Austria, Finland and Sweden

Meeting of the European Convention

Revival of the European project

Against this background, the then German Minister for Foreign Affairs, Hans-Dietrich Genscher, launched a new European initiative at the beginning of the 1980s to define the "European Union" by enshrining it in a "European Act." Towards the end of 1981, the German and Italian governments presented their joint proposals, known as the Genscher-Colombo initiative, which, after a difficult set of negotiations, were quietly forgotten.

Second attempt at a constitution: the Spinelli draft

In the middle of the 1980s, there was another attempt to produce a constitution, this time by the institutional committee of the European Parliament (EP) under the chairmanship of an Italian, Altiero Spinelli, which drew up a draft constitution to establish the European Union.

In June 1979, the first European Parliament to be directly elected by EU citizens convened, conferring a new legitimacy and confidence on its members. However, this confidence could not win over national governments. Although a majority voted in favor of the Spinelli draft in February 1984, it found little support in the national parliaments of the ten member states.

Southern enlargement to include Greece, Portugal and Spain

Although a further deepening of the EC was out of the question for the time being, the European summit at Fontainebleau in June 1984 cleared the way for southern enlargement. Greece had joined in 1981, and now Spain and Portugal signed the accession treaties. Thus, in 1986, the EC had twelve member states.

In the mid 1980s, the then German Chancellor Helmut Kohl and French President François Mitterrand increased the pressure on other EC members by declaring that their countries would pursue the goal of political union even if others weren't yet prepared to follow them.

In the middle of 1985, the European Council meeting in Milan agreed to convene an intergovernmental conference, within which the existing proposals for reform were to be defined and adopted.

Intergovernmental Conference

Intergovernmental conferences are negotiations between member states that are especially important for European integration. They are the forums in which member states and the Commission can submit proposals to the Council of Ministers demanding reforms in the EU institutions. In the past 20 years, there have been at short intervals a whole series of intergovernmental conferences. These have led to the Single European Act (SEA), the Treaties of Maastricht, Amsterdam and Nice, and the Treaty establishing a Constitution for Europe.

At the end of an intergovernmental conference, the Heads of State and Government decide unanimously whether or not to amend the treaties. After a new treaty has been formally signed, it must, in accordance with the varying constitutional arrangements in different member states, be adopted by the parliaments of the member states and/or by the electorate in a referendum. A treaty can only come into force when it has been ratified by every country in the EU.

However, there is an important drawback to intergovernmental conferences. During negotiations each country tries to represent its interests, so that in the end it is often possible to agree on the lowest common denominator reforms only. This was one of the reasons why, rather than draft a treaty themselves, the EU governments agreed to institute a Convention (see Chapter 4.1), the object of which was to prepare a treaty reform. And this then led on to the Constitution.

The decision whether or not to adopt the draft Constitution still rested with the Heads of State and Government. Though the "Convention method" can probably still be improved, it has been a success, and is likely to be used in any future attempts to reform the Treaties.

1985: First reform of the Treaties of Rome

Amendments to the Treaties of Rome were adopted at the Luxembourg summit in December 1985 and legally laid down in what became known as the Single European Act, which took effect on July 1, 1997. The most important amendments included the introduction of majority decisions in the Council of Ministers and the extension of the co-decision rights of the European Parliament.

The requirement for unanimous decisions in central policy areas under the EEC Treaty made it very difficult to complete the internal market. Majority decisions, which were obviously easier to reach, were supposed to overcome the problem.

The Single European Act re-activated the European integration project and motivated European policymakers to continue the completion of the internal market in the framework of the single market project, "Europe '92."

Delors Report on EMU

In the summer of 1988 the European Council commissioned the then President of the European Commission, Jacques Delors, to submit a report on the state of the Economic and Monetary Union (EMU). In June 1989, the Heads of State and Government of what were now twelve EC states decided in Madrid to implement the EMU on the basis of the proposals contained in the Delors report.

Its most important proposals included the irrevocable fixing of exchange rates, the replacement of national currencies by a single currency and the establishment of an independent institution to supervise monetary policy, which later became the European Central Bank.

The fall of the Berlin Wall at the end of the 1980s and the ensuing political changes in the 1990s finally confronted Europe with a completely new set of challenges.

Jacques Delors, President of the Commission from 1985 to 1995

2.3 Marathon-style reforms of the European Treaties in the 1990s

Epoch-making event: the fall of the Berlin Wall

The demise of communism meant that the new nation-states in central and eastern Europe turned their attention to the European Community which, on account of its economic attractiveness and political strength, became a magnet for the whole of Europe.

Faced with the forthcoming enlargement and deepening at the beginning of the 1990s, the European Community was at first confronted with a pile of unfinished business. Over the next few years, the EU began to take on the appearance of a building site. Though this ushered in a new dynamic among EU politicians, citizens failed to notice the changes.

Maastricht 1991: second reform of the Treaties of Rome

In December 1991, another reform of the Treaties of Rome was finalized at Maastricht, and February 1992 saw the signing of the "Treaty on European Union." The European Community, which had previously been based on the economy, was transformed. Under the umbrella of the new EU Treaty, it was now to have a Common Foreign and Security Policy (CFSP), and would cooperate in Justice and Home Affairs.

The ratification of the Maastricht Treaty was a difficult and protracted affair in most EU countries. Three countries held popular referenda: Ireland and France voted in favor of the Treaty, whereas the Danes rejected it in the first public vote on the issue. The Treaty establishing the European Union came into force by the end of 1993, a year late, after the Danes, who had secured certain "opt-outs," voted in favor of it in a second referendum.

New tasks for the EU

After the Maastricht Treaty went into effect, two steps became particularly important: the completion of the Economic and Monetary Union, and a greater involvement of the European Parliament in the European decision-making processes. Member states also agreed to develop a Common Foreign and Security Policy.

Justice and Home Affairs policies were fleshed out on asylum, immigration and visa policies, cooperation by the courts and the police in civil and criminal matters, and the joint fight against terrorism, drug trafficking and international crime. It was also agreed to establish a European police force (Europol). While the Treaty of Maastricht extended cooperation within the framework of the EU to a number of new areas, it failed to bring about political union.

Amsterdam 1997: a new attempt at treaty reform

The dizzying momentum of integration led to an agreement at Maastricht that European Treaties should be scrutinized to see if additional amendments were required. This happened in Amsterdam in 1997, though here again, a dramatic breakthrough did not materialize.

Key problems relating to enlargement in central and eastern Europe such as the Commission's size and composition and vote weighting for member states in the Council of Ministers were left unsolved. These points were subsequently dealt with in another set of amendments to the Treaties. Reforming the "leftovers," as they were called, turned out to be incredibly difficult, since the number of votes in the Council and the representation of the Commission are not simply technical matters. The extent to which a country is represented in the work of EU bodies and the basis on which decisions are made determines its influence in the European Union.

1995: Austria, Finland and Sweden join the EU

The countries of the European Free Trade Area (EFTA), Austria, Finland and Sweden, joined the EU in 1995, which then turned towards the east. European agreements were signed with the states of central and eastern Europe, which meant that an accession to the European Union was just around the corner. The prospect of EU membership also had a moral dimension: the west was offering a route to democracy for nations that had been oppressed by authoritarian regimes.

Since the forthcoming round of EU enlargement would include up to twelve new countries, it was imperative to solve the question of operational viability. The new member states were to participate in the institutions, but without paralyzing them. The Treaty of Amsterdam came into force in May 1999, and the Nice Intergovernmental Conference began soon afterwards in February 2000, at the turn of the millennium. Its task was to prepare the EU for the forthcoming enlargement.

Preparations for enlargement in Nice

The Intergovernmental Conference began under the auspices of the Portuguese Presidency, and was concluded in Nice in December 2000 under the French Presidency. The Treaty of Nice was no success, for it proved impossible to reach satisfactory agreements on most of the important issues—the size and composition of the Commission, the extension of majority decisions in the Council of Ministers, and the revised weighting of votes.

The consensus was once again based on the lowest common denominator. A reduction in the size of the Commission, which was supposed to maintain the viability of the college even when there were 27 and more member states, was adopted in principle, but deferred to a later date. Most countries put up stiff resistance, since they did not wish to relinquish "their" commissioner.

Retention of the veto right

There was also deadlock on the extension of majority decisions in the Council of Ministers. Germany, for example, wished to retain unanimity on asylum and immigration policies, and also managed to secure unanimity on the subject of co-determination and employee participation. Spain refused to relinquish its right of veto with regard to subsidies for structurally weak countries and regions. Britain refused to relinquish its veto on the harmonization of fiscal policy, as did the French in the area of cultural policy.

Vote weighting in the Council of Ministers

The Treaty of Nice also failed to deal with the problem of the weighting of votes of the individual member states in the Council of Ministers. The weighted votes do not accurately reflect the size of the various countries, since their distribution fails to correspond to the actual percentage of the population (small states are in a better position than large ones), and this distorts the political facts.

Furthermore, vote-weighting in the Treaty of Nice forms part of a complicated "triple majority." A majority in the Council of Ministers can materialize only if it comprises a certain number of weighted votes (more than a two-thirds majority) and the majority of the member states, which at the same time must represent 62 percent of the population of the Union (see also Chapter 7.4 and 8.1).

**Structure and Goals of the European Union –
– The "Three-Pillars-Model" in the Treaty of Nice –**

Pillar 1 **European Community**	Pillar 2 **Common Foreign and Security Policy**	Pillar 3 **Police and Judicial Co-operation in Criminal Matters**

• Agricultural policy
• Internal market
• Regional and structural policy
• Social protection and social cohesion
• Environmental protection
• Consumer protection
• Monetary policy
• Competition policy
• Economic development
	• Safeguard common values and interests
	• Strengthen international security
	• Preserve peace
	• Promote international co-operation
	• Develop and consolidate democracy and the rule of law
	• Respect for human rights and fundamental freedoms
		• Create an area of freedom, security and justice
		• Combat:
		  ◦ racism and xenophobia
		  ◦ terrorism
		  ◦ human trafficking
		  ◦ offences against children
		  ◦ illicit drug and arms trafficking
		  ◦ corruption and fraud

The right of veto in the Council of Ministers makes it difficult to reach a decision

The European Treaties stipulate precisely which decisions in the Council of Ministers require unanimity, and which can be reached with a majority vote.

In the areas requiring unanimity, any EU member state can block legislation by exercising its right of veto in the Council of Ministers. This means that, even if a majority of the EU countries is in favor of a certain law, its adoption can be prevented by a single country. The right of veto makes it difficult to reach a decision, particularly in an EU with 27 and more member states.

For this reason, the areas in which unanimity was required had already been curtailed in previous rounds of reform by extending the use of majority decision-making.

Questions of procedure are questions of power

What is the point of such complicated provisions which make it difficult for a majority to materialize? The triple majority devised by the Treaty of Nice is an example of the fact that procedural questions are not simply of a technical nature: they determine the balance of power among sovereign states. For this reason, changes made to this balance are always a highly sensitive issue. They are hotly contested and lead repeatedly to complicated rules which the electorate finds difficult to understand.

The media and many experts on European affairs were critical of what was achieved in Nice, since they had the impression that the participants had lost sight of the real goal, which was to prepare the European institutions for southern and eastern enlargement. However, in truth, the EU had made some progress in the Treaty of Nice, but not enough. The Treaty of Nice contained some important innovations. Thus, for example, it expanded the instrument of → enhanced cooperation, which permits EU states in favor of integration to cooperate more closely without making it necessary for other member states to join them ("Two-speed Europe").

Another successful feature of the Intergovernmental Conference was the adoption of an EU Charter of Fundamental Rights, which had been drawn up by a convention chaired by the former German President, Roman Herzog. The Charter listed for the first time the rights of EU citizens in a systematic manner. Although solemnly proclaimed in Nice, it was not incorporated into a legally binding document.

Adoption of the EU Charter of Fundamental Rights

One of the decisions made in Nice was destined to be of great importance for the future. As a result of an Italo-German initiative, a declaration was appended to the Treaty, the purpose of which was to initiate a wide-ranging dialogue about the legal status of the Charter of Fundamental Rights, a more precise assignment of competences to the EU and the member states, the role of the national parliaments in the institutional architecture of Europe, and the simplification of the existing Treaties. The "post-Nice process," which began with this declaration, formed the basis for the work on the Constitutional Treaty. Until this comes into effect, the Treaty of Nice will continue to be the legal basis of the EU.

Italo-German initiative to save the reforms

2.4 XXL Europe

The accession process began to gather speed in the 1990s. A decision to commence accession negotiations with the Czech Republic, Cyprus, Estonia, Hungary, Poland and Slovenia was made in Luxembourg at the end of 1997, and with Bulgaria, Latvia, Lithuania, Malta, Romania and Slovakia in Helsinki in December 1999. Here, Turkey received the status of an accession candidate.

Accession negotiations with ten eastern European states, Malta and Cyprus

Negotiations went ahead smoothly, with the exception of those with Bulgaria and Romania where internal political and legal reforms had not reached EU standards.

In October 2002, the Commission recommended the accession of ten new countries. After acrimonious debates about how this would be financed, negotiations were finally concluded in Copenhagen in December 2002. The Accession Treaty was signed at a ceremony on the Acropolis in Athens in April 2003, and on May 1, 2004, the Czech Republic, Cyprus, Estonia, Hungary, Latvia, Lithuania, Malta, Poland, Slovakia and Slovenia became members of the EU. Bulgaria and Romania followed in January 2007.

Members of the European Union after 2004

2004 (25 members) Accession of Cyprus, Czech Republic, Estonia, Hungary, Latvia, Lithuania, Malta, Poland, Slovakia and Slovenia

2007 (27 members) Accession of Bulgaria and Romania

Towards the end of 2004, the Heads of State and Government, after much hesitation, also agreed to start accession negotiations with Turkey. These commenced on October 3, 2005. Negotiations with Croatia began at the same time. In December 2005, Macedonia became an official accession candidate.

Negotiations with Turkey and Croatia

A controversial question: Should Turkey join the EU?

Many EU citizens are unhappy about the decision to start accession negotiations with Turkey. Turkey, one of the poorest countries in Europe, would become the EU's most populous and fastest-growing country. The prospect of Turkey joining was a major factor in the referenda in both France and the Netherlands. Prior to the vote, President Jacques Chirac changed the French Constitution to provide that any new entrant after Bulgaria, Romania and Croatia must be approved by a referendum in France. Austria has also promised a vote on Turkey, and other countries may yet join them.

Many EU citizens believe that they should not shoulder the financial burdens that Turkish membership would bring, and they fear the cultural and religious differences between Turkey and the present EU member states.

One answer to such anxieties might be the argument that the integration of an Islamic nation into the EU would promote understanding between different civilizations. If Turkey is not permitted to join the EU, it might begin to take its bearings from the Islamic and Arab world, where democracy and human rights tend to play a subordinate role. By moving closer to the EU, Turkey has undertaken to respect western values and press on with its internal reforms.

Where do Europe's borders end? The last round of enlargement extended the borders of the EU to Ukraine, to the Balkans, and to the Mediterranean. The accession negotiations with Turkey makes it seem that Europe has no borders, and people have begun to ask whether in the near future states such as Ukraine, Morocco, Israel, Palestine, or even Russia and the Caucasus countries will be eligible for membership. If this were to occur, the EU would have as its immediate neighbors countries in a state of crisis.

Close EU partnerships with neighboring states

Even assuming they fulfill the criteria for membership, could the EU in the short to medium term cope with the accession of states with huge populations such as Turkey or poor countries such as the Ukraine or the Republic of Moldova? Currently, this seems unlikely—partly due to internal developments in these countries, and partly due to the EU's lack of further capacity for integration.

Therefore, in addition to the concept of membership, the EU needs to develop a neighborhood policy that is both attractive for the adjoining states and realistic for the Union. An alternative to full membership could, for example, be a new kind of strategic partnership. Future security and stability within the Union and in its immediate neighborhood will depend on this.

The Constitutional Treaty stipulates that the European Union should develop a special relationship with neighboring countries, aiming to establish an area of prosperity and good neighborliness. For this purpose, the Union may conclude specific agreements with the countries without offering the prospect of immediate membership.

3 The path leading to the Constitution

The EU has grown both in terms of its geographical size—from six founding states to its current 27 members—and in terms of the tasks it is required to perform. Whilst it is true that its institutions and decision-making procedures have been improved, the "jungle of treaties" currently in force gives a very tangled picture of the position of the EU's legal basis.

The member states were all of the opinion that, after the large-scale treaty reforms of the past two decades (Single European Act, Treaties of Maastricht, Amsterdam and Nice), there was a need for another fundamental treaty revision.

Treaty overhaul

In the most recent rounds of reform → intergovernmental conferences had made it possible for governments to protect their own interests, which mitigated against far-reaching reforms. Many of the compromises that were struck quickly turned out to be obsolete in practice. Yet, attempts to find a common ground are necessary: political systems require a fundamental consensus about their purpose, their goals, and their structure.

Following insufficient progress in the past rounds of reform, the EU's political system was badly in need of a complete overhaul.

More transparency for EU citizens

The politics of the European Union had to become more transparent and less complicated. The EU itself had to become more democratic, viable and efficient, and had to speak with one voice in foreign policy while making its weight felt in the world. Steps toward a political union, which had failed to materialize in earlier reforms, were to succeed in parallel with the greatest enlargement in the history of the EU.

However, it was doubtful whether the intergovernmental conference method, exhausted and incapable of further expansion,

New method of treaty reform: the EU Convention

was still suitable for further reforms of the EU. Member states looked for a new method that would make it possible to implement the reforms that were so badly needed. In the → "post-Nice process," following the 2000 Nice summit, the EU finally embarked on a fundamental revision of its Treaties on the basis of a completely new method of treaty reform. This was to be performed by a body specially instituted by the Heads of State and Government: the → EU Convention (see diagram, p. 43).

Laeken Declaration lists reform questions

The Declaration of Laeken, issued about a year after the Nice summit, drew up a thematic catalogue of almost 60 questions divided into four thematic areas that clarified where reform was needed. At this stage, the possibility that a fundamental revision of the EU Treaties might lead to a constitution was only cautiously hinted at.

EU Reform: the Principal Questions of the "Laeken Declaration"

1. Assignment and definition of competences in the EU and the member states
   a) How can the assignment of tasks be made more transparent?
   b) On what basis and in which areas must the competences be rearranged?
   c) How can an insidious sprawl in European competences be prevented?

2. Simplification of EU legislative instruments
   How can the legislative instruments and the instruments for the implementation of laws be more precisely defined, and their number reduced?

3. More democracy, transparency and efficiency
   a) How can the working methods and the relationship of the three EU institutions—the Commission, the Parliament, and the Council of Ministers—be improved?
   b) What role should the national parliaments play in European politics?

c) How can efficiency and working methods be improved in the light of an EU with about 30 member states?

4. The path towards a constitution
   a) How can the Treaties be simplified without changing their meaning?
   b) What might their revision look like?
   c) How could the Charter of Fundamental Rights be incorporated into a new basic treaty?
   d) Could this mean that the EU might adopt a constitutional text?

4 The genesis of the Constitution

4.1 The European Convention

Convention meets in public

EU states attempted to address flaws in previous intergovernmental negotiations by establishing the Convention for the reform of the European Treaties. There was a deliberate decision to select a completely different set of participants for the EU Convention, which, uniquely, was to meet in public.

Accession states are also represented

The Convention was made up of 105 members and their deputies, and comprised government representatives and members of national parliaments, members of the European Parliament, and members of the Commission. Delegates from the governments and parliaments of the accession states were also represented, though they did not have the right to vote. The Convention was headed by former French President Valéry Giscard d'Estaing. The two vice-presidents were former prime ministers, Giuliano Amato (Italy) and Jean-Luc Dehaene (Belgium).

4.2 Treaty reform with EU citizen participation

Participation of the general public

The reform process was to benefit from a greater degree of civil society involvement from EU citizens. In this way, it was thought that it might be possible to overcome the general lethargy and scepticism about anything to do with Europe. And it was a way of responding to the widespread criticisms that EU politicians did not communicate sufficiently with the people they represent.

There was a special plenary session with representatives of European civil society. The public was invited to become involved

The composition of the EU Convention

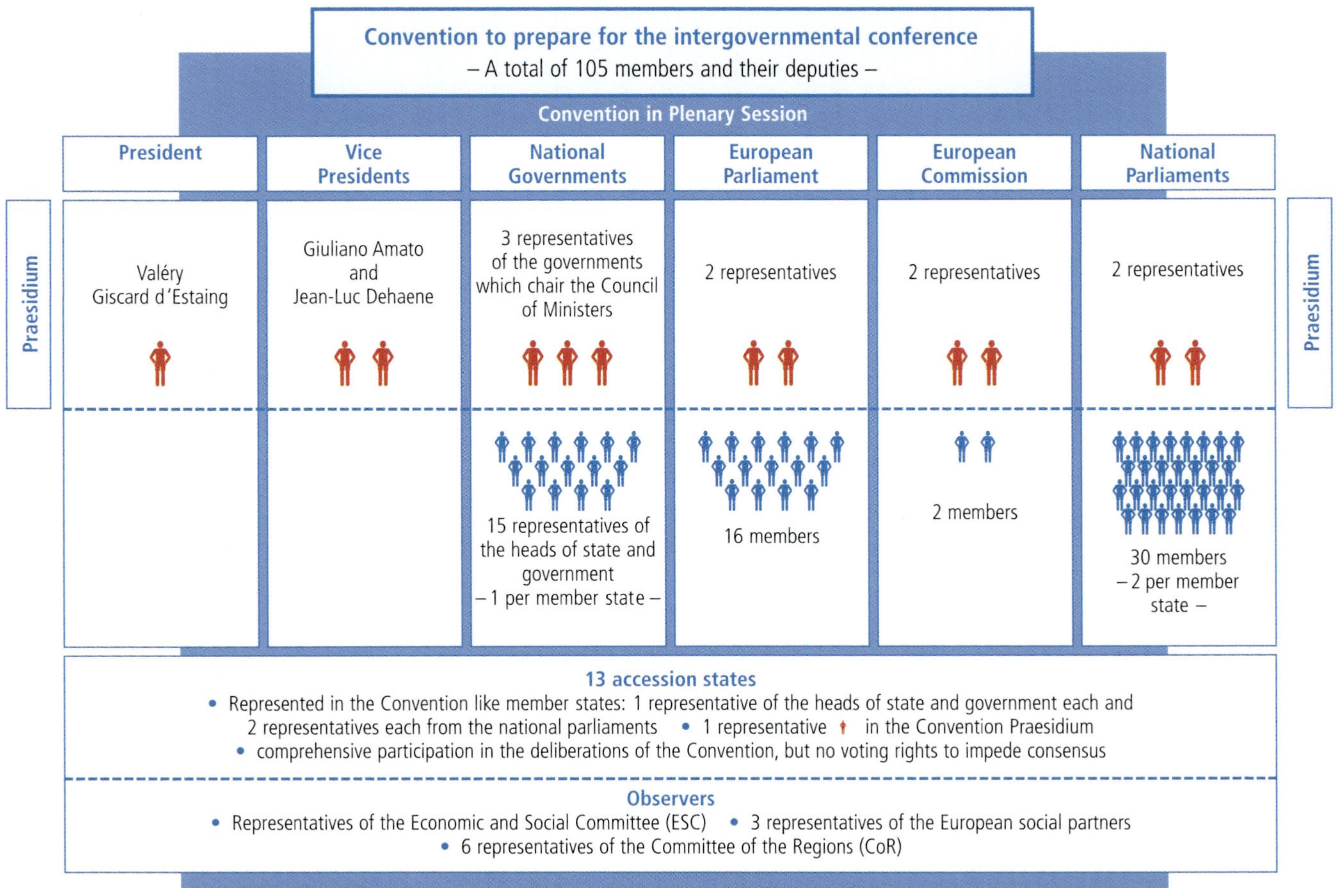

within the framework of an EU Youth Convention, and through "Forum" and "Futurum," two Internet web sites.

Convention openness is a success

This time, the Treaty was not, as in the past, negotiated behind closed doors, but through an open public process. This worked well; conflicts and tactical maneuvers were far more visible than at earlier intergovernmental conferences. Unfortunately, it was difficult for EU citizens to get involved, since they had not been properly informed about the possibility of participating in the Convention process. Many people were not even aware that the Convention existed.

4.3 Chronology of the constitutional process

Draft Constitution took only 17 months to complete

The new round of reforms began to pick up speed after the Laeken Declaration in December 2001, and the Convention began its work at the end of February 2002. A twelve-member praesidium and eleven working groups, each of which was devoted to a particular topic, managed to produce in only 17 months what few had thought possible: a single constitutional text that was presented to the Italian Presidency on July 18, 2003. In accordance with the stipulations governing amendments to the Treaties, this draft now had to be presented for approval to an intergovernmental conference.

Start of the Intergovernmental Conference

The Intergovernmental Conference, which had the task of approving the final version of the Constitutional Treaty, began on October 4, 2003 under the auspices of the Italian Presidency. It included participants from the ten accession states that were due to become members of the EU on May 1, 2004.

Dispute about "double majority" voting

It was now the turn of the member states that were dissatisfied with some of the results that had emerged from the Convention process. The debate was primarily about the new voting procedures in the Council of Ministers, the → "double majority." Poland and Spain were vehemently opposed to this, since they felt that, compared to their position in the Treaty of Nice, they were now being unfairly treated. The Treaty of Nice stipulates that a triple majority is required in the case of majority decisions in the Council of Ministers, i.e., a majority of the EU population, a majority of member states and a majority of the weighted votes.

The Draft Constitution is presented to the Italian Presidency

Concerning the latter, Spain and Poland each had 27 votes, whereas Germany, France, the United Kingdom and Italy, which are more populous countries, only had 29—a disparity that might lead to a political imbalance. Poland and Spain held that they were better off with the Nice rules and wanted to retain them at all costs. But the double majority of the Constitutional Treaty sought to abolish this voting criterion.

Setback during the Intergovernmental Conference

Before the adoption of the Constitutional Treaty in June 2004, Europe witnessed some dramatic moments. In December 2003, the constitutional summit in Brussels ended in a failure primarily on account of the issue of the → "double majority" in the Council of Ministers. Spain and Poland refused to accept the changes to the Treaty of Nice, Germany and France were unwilling to compromise, and the Italian Presidency under the leadership of Silvio Berlusconi was unable to mediate between the two.

For the time being, it seemed as if Europe's hopes of adopting a European Constitution had been dashed. There was a general feeling of disappointment and mutual recriminations. The then German Foreign Minister Joschka Fischer accused the then British Foreign Secretary Jack Straw of trying to "salami slice" the Constitution. Straw claimed that the negotiating chamber was full of "mosquitos trying to bite the British." It was, in fact, highly uncertain whether the Constitution would ever be adopted. How-

June 1997	In Amsterdam the heads of state and government agree that reforms are needed (e.g., a smaller Commission, weighted votes in the Council) on account of EU enlargement.
December 2000	Treaty of Nice, "Declaration on the Future of the Union" with four main areas of reform (re-arrangement of competences, Charter of Fundamental Rights, inclusion of national parliaments, simplification of the Treaties); the Swedish and Belgian Presidencies of the Council are commissioned to organize the "post-Nice process," and an exchange of views on these subjects with the participation of the European Commission, the European Parliament, the national parliaments, and EU citizens.
December 2001	European Council in Laeken, "Declaration of Laeken" with 57 questions in four blocks (assignment and definition of competences, simplification of instruments, more democracy, transparency, and efficiency); decision to institute a Convention headed by Valéry Giscard d'Estaing to prepare for an Intergovernmental Conference.
February 2002	The Convention begins its deliberations. As a whole it meets on 27 occasions. Eleven working groups and three discussion circles are set up: • Working Group I . . . . . Subsidiarity • Working Group II . . . . . Charter of Fundamental Rights • Working Group III . . . . . Legal Personality • Working Group IV . . . . . National Parliaments • Working Group V . . . . . Complementary Competences • Working Group VI . . . . . Economic Governance • Working Group VII . . . . . External Action • Working Group VIII . . . . . Defence • Working Group IX . . . . . Simplification • Working Group X . . . . . Freedom, Security, and Justice • Working Group XI . . . . . Social Europe

constitutional process

• Discussion Circle I .... European Court of Justice • Discussion Circle II .... Budgetary Procedure • Discussion Circle III .... Own Resources	
European Council in Thessalonika. Presentation of the draft Constitution by the President of the Convention, Giscard d'Estaing (Parts I, II, and IV of the draft).	**June 2003**
Convention discusses the conclusions of the European Council in Thessalonika and completes work on Part IV; the final draft is signed by the members of the Convention and presented to the Italian Presidency.	**July 2003**
The Intergovernmental Conference which must decide whether or not to adopt the draft Constitution begins.	**October 2003**
European Council meets in Brussels. The heads of state and government are unable to reach agreement on the draft Constitution. This is primarily due to the question of the "double majority" (states and population) voting procedure in the Council of Ministers. A decision is deferred.	**December 2003**
European Council meets in Brussels. A decision is taken to resume negotiations.	**March 2004**
European Council meets in Brussels. All 25 member states reach agreement on the Constitutional Treaty. The Intergovernmental Conference concludes by adopting the "Treaty establishing a Constitution for Europe".	**June 2004**
Constitutional Treaty solemnly signed by all the heads of state and government on Capitol Hill in Rome, start of the ratification process in the member states.	**October 2004**

ever, politicians were well aware of the fact that the failure of the constitutional process would have serious consequences. The opportunity to establish a stable and common foundation for a Europe consisting of 27 or more states would have been squandered and would not present itself again for the foreseeable future.

Constitutional Treaty is adopted

After the failure of the summit in December 2003, negotiations on the European Constitution were resumed early in 2004 under the Irish EU Presidency. It proved possible to broker a compromise, and on June 18, 2004, the EU Constitution was adopted after all.

Certain aspects of this compromise were retrogressive when compared to the draft prepared by the Convention. However, it was the only way in which agreement could be reached. Even if the Constitution in its final form is a long way from being perfect, it offers clear advantages when compared to the Treaty of Nice, which is currently in force.

5 The structure of the Constitution

Condensing the European Treaties

The Treaties currently in force, which comprise the EC Treaty, the EU Treaty, and numerous protocols and declarations, were restructured by the Convention and combined in the form of a single document. More than 700 articles of the European Treaties have been whittled down to 448.

Constitution consists of four parts

The Treaty establishing a Constitution for Europe (TCE) consists of four parts (see table, p. 53). Part I describes the basic provisions concerning the goals, values, competences and institutions of the EU. Part II contains the Charter of Fundamental Rights, which was compiled under the chairmanship of former German President Roman Herzog (see table, pp. 50–51). Part III elaborates on Part I and contains particular regulations pertaining to the institutions and policy areas. Part IV contains the concluding provisions.

Should God be mentioned?

The Constitution is preceded by a preamble in which the EU member states undertake to respect human dignity, freedom, democracy, equality and the rule of law. One of the most contentious issues among the member states was whether to include an explicit reference to God in the Preamble. Poland, with support from Italy, Spain and Ireland, wanted it included. There were equally strong secular concerns voiced by France, Denmark and assorted liberals and socialists from across Europe, who argued that republican ideals demanded a separation of religion and the state. Supporters of a reference to God brought up historical arguments that worried secularists—particularly given the diverse Muslim, Hindu and Jewish populations of most European countries. An explicit reference to Europe as a "Christian Club" could, it was feared, further alienate Muslims at a time of tension.

The European Charter of Fundamental Rights – Part II of the EU Constitution

The Charter has 54 articles and includes the following fundamental rights:

At the top of the agenda: Respect for human dignity

Article II-61: Human dignity

Human dignity is inviolable. It must be respected and protected.

Article II-62: Right to life

Everyone has the right to life.
No one shall be condemned to the death penalty or executed.

Freedoms

Article II-70: Freedom of thought, conscience and religion

Everyone has the right to freedom of thought, conscience and religion.

Article II-71: Freedom of expression and information

Everyone has the right to freedom of expression.
This right shall include freedom to hold opinions and
to receive and import information
and ideas without interference by public authority and
regardless of frontiers.

Article II-72: Freedom of assembly and of association

Everyone has the right to freedom of peaceful assembly and
to freedom of association at all levels, in particular in political, trade union and
civic matters, which implies the right of everyone to form and
to join trade unions for the protection of his or her interests.

Article II-79: Protection in the event of removal, expulsion or extradition

Collective expulsions are prohibited. No one may be removed, expelled or extradited
to a State where there is a serious risk that he or she would be punished
to the death penalty, torture or other inhuman or degrading treatment or punishment.

Equality

Article II-80: Equality before the law

Everyone is equal before the law.

Article II-81: Non-discrimination

Any discrimination based on any ground such as sex, race, colour, ethnic or
social origin, genetic features, language, religion or belief, political or
any other opinion, membership of a national minority, property, birth,
disability, age or sexual orientation shall be prohibited.

Article II-83: Equality between women and men

Equality between men and women must be ensured in all areas,
including employment, work and pay.

Solidarity and environmental protection

Article II-91: Fair and just working conditions

Every worker has the right to working conditions which respect his or her health, safety and dignity. Every worker has the right to limitation of maximum working hours, to daily and weekly rest periods and to an annual period of paid leave.

Artikel II-97: Environmental protection

A high level of environmental protection and the improvement of the quality of the environment must be integrated into the policies of the Union and ensured in accordance with the principle of sustainable development.

Citizens' rights in the Charter

Article II-99: Right to vote and to stand as a candidate at elections to the European Parliament

Every citizen of the Union has the right to vote and to stand as a candidate at elections to the European Parliament in the member state in which he or she resides, under the same conditions as nationals of the State.

Article II-100: Right to vote and to stand as a candidate at municipal elections

Every citizen of the Union has the right to vote and to stand as a candidate at municipal elections in the member state in which he or she resides under the same conditions as nationals of that State.

Article II-106: Diplomatic and consular protection

Every citizen of the Union shall, in the territory of a third country in which the member state of which he or she is a national is not represented, be entitled to protection by the diplomatic or consular authorities of any member state, on the same conditions as the nationals of that member state.

Justice

Article II-108: Presumption of innocence and right of defence

Everyone who has been charged shall be presumed innocent until proved guilty according to law.

Article II-110: Right not to be tried or punished twice in criminal proceedings for the same criminal offence

No one shall be liable to be tried or punished again in criminal proceedings for an offence for which he or she has already been finally acquitted or convicted within the Union in accordance with the law.

Here again, it proved possible to strike a compromise. Instead of referring directly to God or to Europe's Christian heritage, the Preamble refers to its religious, cultural and humanist inheritance.

Charter of Fundamental Rights: Europe as a value-based community

The Charter (Part II) makes it easier for the individual to understand his or her fundamental rights, since it lists the rights of EU citizens and important common values and convictions, and thus creates legal security. Precisely because European laws and institutions are beginning to affect the daily lives of EU citizens, it is especially important to guarantee European fundamental rights. Here, the Constitution would provide full protection for the fundamental rights of EU citizens.

For future member states, respect for the principles of the rule of law constitutes a basic precondition for EU membership. The Charter makes it clear throughout the world that the European Union attaches great importance to fundamental and human rights. Europe now presents itself to the world as a community with shared values and a sense of belonging.

Opposition to the Charter

However, the Charter ran into strong opposition. In Britain, opponents argued that it would give greater scope for judges to override British laws, though there was not significant opposition from other countries. Opponents also worried that the protection of the "right to strike" would overturn Margaret Thatcher's Trade Union reforms of the 1980s, and that rights to "collective bargaining" and workers' rights to "information and consultation" would damage economic competitiveness. Eventually, in return for defending the right to veto on tax harmonization, the British Government accepted the measure and pinned their hopes on a statement stressing it would apply only "to the member states when they are implementing EU law" and that it should only be applied according to national traditions.

In response, the French complained that this destroyed the Charter's ability to promote the "social Europe" agenda. However, only following a series of court judgements, will it be clear exactly how the Charter will be interpreted. Despite the caveats now added to the Charter, it could have an impact on domestic policy. For instance, France's famous ban on the headscarf in schools could be challenged on the grounds that it bans the parents' rights to see their children educated "in conformity with their religious, philosophical and pedagogical convictions."

The basic structure of the EU Constitution

Preamble

Part I	Part II	Part III	Part IV
Basic provisions, competences and institutions of the Union – 60 articles –	**Charter of Fundamental Rights** – 54 articles –	**The Policies and Functioning of the Union** – 322 articles –	**General and Final Provisions** – 12 articles –
Title I Definition and Objectives **Title II** Fundamental Rights and Citizenship of the Union **Title III** Competences **Title IV** Institutions and Bodies **Title V** Exercise of Competence **Title VI** Democratic Life **Title VII** Finances **Title VIII** The Union and its Neighbours **Title IX** Union Membership	Separate Preamble **Title I** Human Dignity **Title II** Freedoms **Title III** Equality **Title IV** Solidarity **Title V** Citizens' Rights **Title VI** Justice **Title VII** General Provisions Governing the Interpretation and Application of the Charter	**Title I** Provisions of General Application **Title II** Non-discrimination and Citizenship **Title III** Internal Policies and Action **Title IV** Association of the Overseas Countries and Territories **Title V** The Union's External Action **Title VI** The Functioning of the Union **Title VII** Common Provisions	• Repeal of Earlier Treaties • Succession and Legal Continuity • Transitional Provisions relating to certain Institutions • Scope • Regional Unions • Protocols and Annexes • Ordinary Revision Procedure • Simplified Revision Procedure • Simplified Revision Procedure concerning internal Union Policies and Action • Duration • Ratification and Entry into Force • Authentic Texts and Translations

Appended are 36 protocols and 50 declarations

Part III of the Constitutional Treaty: long and complicated

Part III, with its more than 300 articles, is the longest section of the Constitution. It consists primarily of legislation from the EC Treaty in the version adopted in Nice that is already in force. The regulations were rearranged in the Constitution, which contains detailed provisions on EU citizenship (for example, a ban on discrimination, the right to vote and to run as a candidate at elections to the European Parliament and at municipal elections, and diplomatic and consular protection). Furthermore, there are detailed provisions concerning the various European policy areas such as the internal market, economic and monetary policy, employment and social policy, agriculture, environment, consumer protection, energy and transport, regulations governing the institutions of the Union, and financial provisions.

On account of its detailed provisions, Part III is a difficult text to read. Some experts suggested taking the detailed provisions out of the actual constitutional text itself, which would have made it easier to understand. However, their suggestions went unheeded. As a result, it has proven impossible to compile a constitutional document expressed in language that the electorate can understand.

Part IV regulates the abolition of earlier treaties, various procedures for future amendments to the Constitutional Treaty, and contains provisions relating to the Constitution's entry into force.

Appendix with 36 protocols and 50 declarations

The complexity of the Constitution is compounded by the fact that the appendix of the new EU basic legal document contains numerous protocols (36) and declarations (50). The protocols relate, for example, to the role of national parliaments, to amendments to the Euratom Treaty, but also to regulating the application of the principles of subsidiarity and proportionality, and declarations on numerous articles of the Constitution. In the protocols, various regulations are more precisely defined and elucidated than in the constitutional text itself.

The appendix is almost as long as the four parts of the Constitution that precede it, making it complex and difficult to read. However, it is not unusual to append protocols and declarations to a treaty, to leave certain questions unresolved and to introduce special regulations in order to be able to reach agreement since all EU states have to ratify the new Treaty before it can be adopted and come into force.

6 EU competences: Who does what?

Clear division of competences between the member states and the EU

In the Constitution, the assignment of "legislative competences" to the member states and the European Union is more defined than ever before. However, this does not signify the foundation of a European state or the complete loss of sovereignty of member states. The opposite is true. The intention has been, in fact, to remove the ambiguities surrounding the division of competences between the EU, the member states and other state actors, such as, for example, the Scottish Parliament or the German Federal States.

A clear definition of which level would perform a specific task has been a long-term goal pursued by Britain. The loss of power to "Brussels" has been the central cause of British Eurosceptics for a generation—and it is only the principle of subsidiarity that has allowed pro-Europeans to counter their claims. The division of competences (see table, p. 57) attained in the Constitutional Treaty is designed as a safeguard that will produce greater transparency and democratic control over European governance.

The EU cannot exercise competences of its own accord

The British Constitution has never been codified, and the separation of powers between different institutions is as much a matter of precedent as accumulated law. Likewise, the European Treaties currently in force have never been presented in a single document. Until now, there has merely been what is known as the "principle of conferral." Thus, the EU cannot of its own accord begin to exercise certain competences, since the member states must first define them precisely and confer them on the Union.

But in practice, it is often difficult to decide whether the European Union has acted within its designated powers or has gone beyond them. The Constitution stipulates that only those competences conferred on the Union in the Constitutional Treaty are its responsibility. All other competences remain with the member states.

6.1 Exclusive EU competence

Only the EU is permitted to adopt legally binding acts

The exclusive responsibilities of the European Union are set out in Article I-12. In this competence category, only the EU is permitted to adopt legally binding acts. The member states may legislate in this area only if they have been empowered to do so by the Union or in order to implement EU legislative acts on the national level.

Article I-13 para. 1 lists the various areas of exclusive EU competence. In addition to the customs union, these include the rules of competition in the internal market, monetary policy in the euro zone, the conservation of marine biological resources under the common fisheries policy, and the common commercial policy. Furthermore, the EU has exclusive competence for the conclusion of certain international agreements.

6.2 Areas with shared competence

EU and member states share competences

The areas in which the Union and the member states are both empowered to legislate are set out in Article I-12 para. 2 and Article I-14 of the Constitution. However, the member states can only exercise their competence in these areas to the extent that the Union has not exercised, or has decided to cease exercising, its competence.

The main areas listed are the internal market, social policy (for the aspects defined in Part III), economic, social and territorial cohesion, agriculture and fisheries (excluding the conservation of marine biological resources), environment, consumer protection, transport, trans-European networks, energy, the European area of freedom, security and justice, and common safety concerns in public health matters.

Assignment of competences still ambiguous

In this list there is merely talk of principal areas. The imprecise assignment of responsibilities still persists.

The categories of competence in the Constitution

Exclusive competences

Only the EU is permitted to adopt legally binding acts. The member states may legislate only if they have been empowered to do so by the EU.

Areas:
Customs union, rules of competition in the internal market, monetary policy in the Eurozone, common commercial policy, conservation of marine biological resources (fisheries policy).

Shared competences

Both the EU and member states are empowered to legislate.

Areas:
Internal market, aspects of social policy, structural policy, agriculture and fisheries, environment, consumer protection, transport and trans-European networks, energy, area of freedom, security and justice.

Supporting, coordinating or complementary action

Action which the EU may take without infringing the rights of member states.

Areas:
Industry, culture, tourism, education, youth, sport and vocational training, civil protection, administrative co-operation, protection and improvement of human health.

Co-ordination of economic and employment policies

Measures adopted by the Council of Ministers for the co-ordination of economic, employment, and social policies.

Common Foreign and Security Policy

The EU competence in the Common Foreign and Security Policy covers all areas of foreign policy relating to the security of the EU, including the progressive framing of a common defence policy.

6.3 Supporting, coordinating and complementary action

EU support and coordination

Article I-12 para. 5 and Article I-17 of the Constitution describe action which the European Union can take without superseding the competence of the member states. The list includes the protection and improvement of human health, and the areas of industry, culture, tourism, education, youth, sport and vocational training, civil protection and administrative cooperation.

General evaluation of the European Constitution

Positive		Negative
• Earlier Treaties combined in one document • Legally binding incorporation of the Charter of Fundamental Rights • Conferral of a legal personality on the EU • Clarification of powers between different EU institutions	**Transparency**	• No brief, comprehensible and succinct constitutional document • Important provisions relegated to protocols • Imprecise boundaries between the competences of different EU institutions • Unclear division between legislative Council and other ministerial Councils
• Co-decision procedure as ordinary legislative procedure • Extension of cases in which the co-decision procedure applies • Extension of European Parliament (EP) rights in budgetary procedure • Introduction of a "European citizens' initiative" • Greater EP influence on the election of the President of the Commission	**Democracy**	• European Council has the right to nominate candidate for the office of Commission President if no "genuine" election by the European Parliament • Nomination procedure for commissioners concludes with a majority decision of the European Council and not the European Parliament • No consistent implementation of the principle of degressive proportionality in determining the number of MEPs
• Introduction of "double majority" voting in the Council of Ministers • Extension of qualified majority decision-making • Introduction of a President of the European Council • Establishment of a Union Minister for Foreign Affairs and an External Action Service • Reduction in the number of Commissioners (two-thirds of member states) • Strengthening of the President of the Commission	**Efficiency and political leadership**	• Introduction of additional criteria for "double majority" voting • Majority decisions are not applicable across a wide range of areas including trade, environmental and immigration policies, and Common Foreign and Security Policy • Unclear division of tasks between the President of the European Council, the President of the Commission, and the Union Minister for Foreign Affairs • The Commission is to be reduced only from 2014 onwards
• Reform of the differentiation instrument "Enhanced Co-operation" • New flexibility in security and defence policy • Simplified amendment of specific details of internal policies • Simplified amendment of the decision-making procedure (bridging clause)	**Continued development**	• Unclear what will happen if it proves impossible to ratify the Constitution • Future constitutional reforms will require ratification by all EU states • Constitution is not divided into two parts consisting of constitutional and executive provisions • Enhanced Co-operation in the field of Common Foreign and Security Policy requires unanimity

It is expressly forbidden in all these fields to use EU legislation in order to effect a harmonization of member states' laws or regulations. In these areas the EU's task is merely to support its members.

6.4 Coordination of economic and employment policies

Article I-15 contains provisions relating to the coordination of economic policy, employment policy, and social policy.

6.5 Common Foreign and Security Policy (CFSP)

According to Article I-16 of the Constitution, EU responsibility for the CFSP covers all areas of foreign policy and all questions relating to the security of the EU, including the progressive framing of a common defense policy.

Categories four and five are unusual in that they are not formulated in abstract terms, but refer to specific areas.

Competences need clearer structure

The introduction of competence categories marks the first step towards an orderly assignment of competences. However, the EU Convention and the → Intergovernmental Conference were unable to subject the division of tasks between the European Union and the member states to sufficient scrutiny. The Constitution does not contain a clear and conclusive division of competences.

The shared competences in the various policy areas are described in over 300 articles in Part III of the Treaty, but are not assigned clearly to the categories in Part I. The allocation of competences—together with the question of responsibility, imputability and accountability in European politics—should therefore be made clearer.

7 The EU institutions and their function in the Constitution

Since change will always create institutional winners and losers, decision-making procedures are difficult to reform. However, reform becomes necessary if a political system remains weak or the outside world radically changes. Both of these factors apply to the European Union.

More tasks and more member states

Over the last two decades, member states have conferred more and more tasks on the EU (Internal Market, Monetary Union, Schengen Accords, etc.). However, the EU still does not possess effective decision-making mechanisms. This weakness is compounded by the expansion of the EU from 12 to 27 within a decade.

The political system of the Union was originally designed for a community of six states and was adapted gradually, though without really putting the EU in a position to meet the challenges of the future.

Ready to meet the future after reforming the institutions

The four important treaty reforms in the recent past, from the Single European Act to Maastricht, Amsterdam and Nice, all attempted to solve the institutional problems, though for the most part they ground to a halt without achieving what they set out to do. It was time to tackle the badly-needed institutional reforms.

Strengthening EU institutions

The Constitution provides the institutional system of the European Union with a new kind of architecture (see diagram, p. 62). Every element of the future institutional quadrangle—which consists of the European Commission, the European Council, the Council of Ministers and the European Parliament—has been strengthened. Yet, the interaction of EU institutions continues to be complicated and lacking in transparency due to the fact that the new European architecture of power reflects a compromise between the advocates of a purely interstate and the proponents of a supranational European Union.

What is the new architecture of the Union? What are the main changes to its institutions? And which institutions benefit from the reforms?

7.1 The European Parliament

The Parliament is the Chamber of Citizens

Direct elections to the European Parliament (EP) have been held since 1979. Prior to this, representatives of the national parliaments had simply been seconded to the EP. The EP is elected every five years and, together with the EU Council of Ministers, has a legislative role. It exercises control over the work of the Commission and forms, together with the Council of Ministers, the EU's budgetary authority. There have now been six elections to the European Parliament, the most recent of which was in June 2004. There are currently 785 members of the European Parliament (MEP). The number of MEPs per member state is based on the size of the population and currently lies between 5 (Malta) and 99 (Germany).

What changes does the Constitution introduce with regard to the Parliament?

European Parliament strengthened

Under the Constitutional Treaty the total number of MEPs will be limited to 750. The distribution of seats will lie between 6 and 96. Following on from reforms introduced in Maastricht, Amsterdam, and Nice, the Constitution strengthens the influence of the Parliament in the political system of the EU. Having undergone dynamic development, the Parliament is now again one of the principal beneficiaries of the reforms (see diagram, p. 62).

EP makes decisions on an equal footing with the Council of Ministers

Under the Constitution, greater budgetary rights will be conferred on the Parliament (in conjunction with the Council of Ministers). Until now, the EP has only had the final word in a number of budgetary areas; others have remained the preserve of the Council of Ministers. As a result of the Constitution, the Parliament's budgetary authority will apply to virtually every area. The

The new face of the European Union

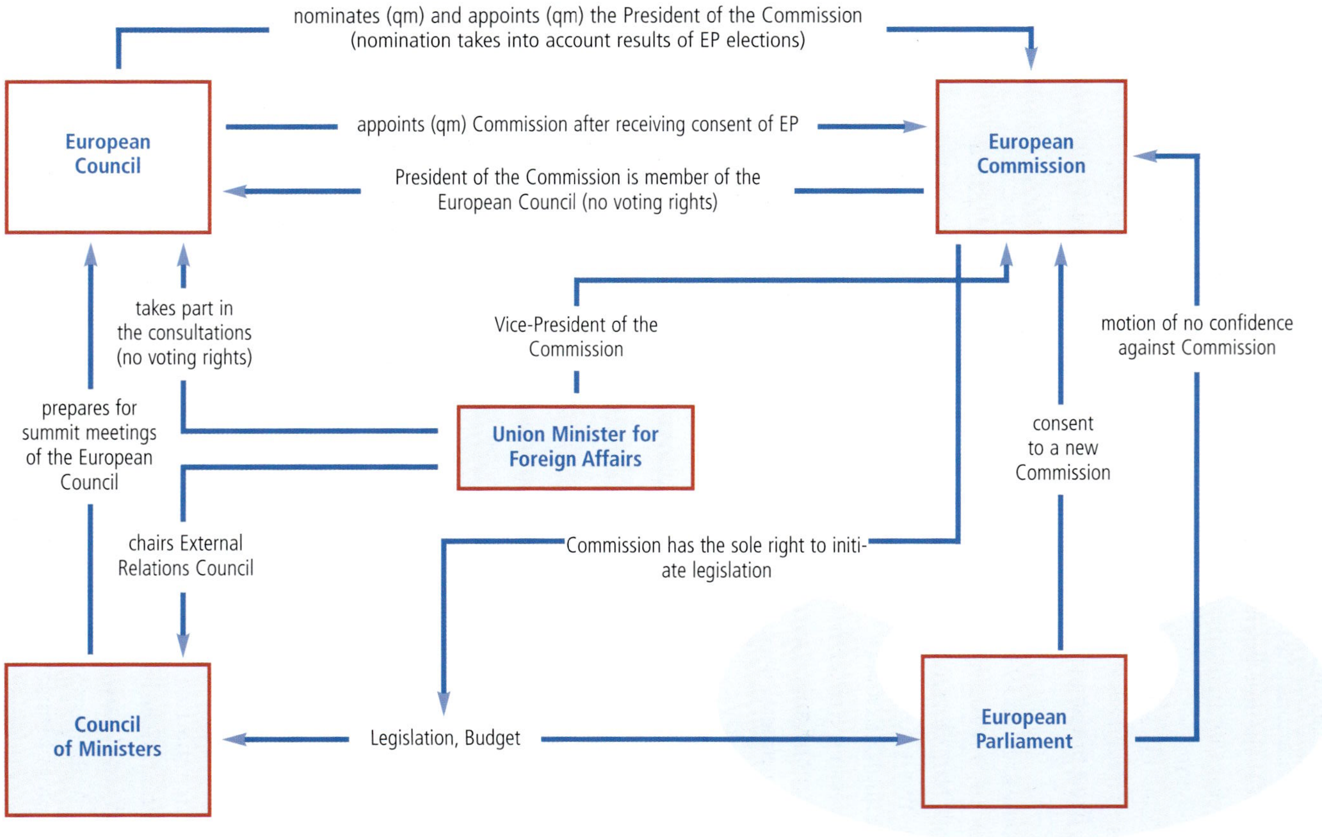

qm: qualified majority

European Parliament is now on an equal footing with the Council of Ministers.

The Parliament has been given a stronger role in the election of the President of the Commission. Until now, the European Parliament gave its consent after the European Council selected a candidate chosen by the Heads of State and Government on the basis of a qualified majority vote. In principle, the member states were free to choose whom they wished. The Constitution stipulates that the European Council must now take its bearings from the political composition of the EP, since it will be appointing a candidate following the outcome of the European elections. Therefore, if the Christian Democrats and Conservatives in the European People's Party (EPP) win the European elections, it is difficult to imagine the European Council ignoring the result and nominating a Social Democrat to be President of the Commission.

The importance of the Parliament is also enhanced on account of the extension of the areas in which the → co-decision procedure is applied. This procedure is the European Parliament's chief instrument of power. It can participate in legislation on an equal footing with the Council of Ministers and, in the final analysis, reject the Commission's legislative initiatives.

Co-decision procedure to be extended

The Constitution states that, in the future, the Parliament will always have co-decision rights in what is known as the "ordinary legislative procedure" for the adoption of European legislative acts whenever a decision is reached in the Council of Ministers on the basis of a qualified majority. This establishes a standard procedure in the European Treaties in which the Council of Ministers and the European Parliament participate on an equal footing.

Although there are still a series of exceptions in which the rights of the Parliament remain weaker, the Constitution has sent out a clear signal that public perceptions should change: the European Parliament is no longer a paper tiger.

More influence for EU citizens

The strengthening of the European Parliament, the only EU institution directly elected by its citizens, increases democratic control of the Union's policies.

The Constitution stipulates that in the case of any future EU enlargement, the Parliament will not increase in size. In order to remain manageable, it will comprise no more than 750 seats.

The European Parliament

European Parliament

- legislates (together with Council of Ministers)
- has budgetary powers
- gives consent to appointment of new Commission
- can pass a motion of no confidence against the Commission
- participates in the continuing development of the Treaties

President
Bureau
– 5 years –

elect

– maximum of 750 MEPs –

- Electoral term: 5 years
- 6 to 96 MEPs per EU Member State
- Multinational parties and political groups, e.g., European People's Party (EPP), Party of European Socialists (PES)
- From 2009 seats assigned on the basis of population size (degressively proportional)

However, it is unfortunate that the EU countries were not able to agree on a binding formula to determine the number of national seats in the Parliament irrespective of further rounds of enlargement. More haggling about the number of national parliamentarians in the European Parliament is inevitable whenever new member states join the EU.

7.2 The European Council

From informal body to principal actor

The meteoric rise of the European Council is remarkable. Planned in the 1970s as an informal fireside chat for the Heads of State and Government and their Ministers for Foreign Affairs, this body has become one of the principal actors in the European Union. Although the European Council has until now been ignored in the European Treaties, it plays an increasingly important role in fundamental decision-making, the establishment of guidelines, and the day-to-day politics of the EU.

As a rule, the European Council meets four times a year. As in the Council of Ministers, the member states rotate the chair twice a year.

"Confusing" Councils

The *European Council* is sometimes confused with the *Council of the European Union* and also with the *Council of Europe*—three completely different institutions.

The *European Council* refers to the regular meetings of the Heads of State and Government, including the President of the European Commission, which take place since 1974. They are also known as "summits."

The *Council of the European Union*, also referred to in abbreviated form simply as Council, refers to the Council of Ministers of the EU.

The *Council of Europe* is an international organization with members from European states that is devoted to the defense of democracy, human rights, the rule of law, the common cultural heritage and the promotion of social progress. Currently, the Council of Europe has 46 members. The United States, Canada, Japan, Mexico and the Vatican possess observer status. Ten members, including Britain, founded the Council of Europe, which is located in Strasbourg, in 1949. *The Council of Europe is not an EU institution.*

What changes does the Constitution introduce with regard to the European Council?

Apart from the European Parliament, the European Council has benefited most from the Constitution. It is listed, for the first time, as the second in order of institutional pre-eminence behind the European Parliament (and therefore before the Council of Ministers, the Commission and the European Court of Justice) (see diagram, p. 67). The European Council forms the fourth corner of an institutional quadrangle and complements the existing triangle (consisting of Council of Ministers, Parliament and Commission).

Constitution strengthens the European Council

Its tasks range from the right to nominate a candidate for the President of the Commission; the election of the Union's Minister for Foreign Affairs; the transfer of certain empowerments to the ordinary legislative procedure or to qualified majority decision-making, to the right to make decisions in the area of the Common Foreign and Security Policy.

In the future, the European Council is to meet at least four times a year together with the → Union's Minister for Foreign Affairs. The President of the European Council and the President of the Commission are not eligible to vote in the European Council.

7.3 The President of the European Council

New: the President of the European Council

With the enlargement of the EU to 27 member states, the six-monthly rotation of the Presidency has become unworkable. Thus, the Constitution proposes its abolition and replacement by a → permanent President of the European Council to give it strategic direction. He or she is elected by the European Council with qualified majority for a period of two-and-a-half years (and can be re-elected once). The President may not hold a national office. This means, for example, that a British Prime Minister or a French President cannot simultaneously be President of the European Council.

The President coordinates the work of the European Council and prepares for the EU summits. The President of the European

The European Council
and the President of the European Council

The European Council

Composition

- The heads of state and government; the President of the Commission (no voting rights)
- The Union Minister for Foreign Affairs attends the meetings of the European Council

Principal tasks

- Determines political directions and priorities
- Holds four meetings a year (plus other de facto meetings)
- Does not exercise legislative functions
- Elects the President of the European Council (qm)
- Appoints the Union Minister for Foreign Affairs (qm)
- Nominates (qm) and appoints (qm) the President of the
- Commission

elects with qualified majority

chairs, provides impetus

The President of the European Council

- Two-and-a-half-year term of office
- Can be re-elected once
- Barred from holding a national office
- Receives support from the General Secretariat of the Council of Ministers

Tasks

- Represents the EU externally (notwithstanding the powers of the Union Minister for Foreign Affairs)
- Prepares for meetings of the European Council
- Chairs the European Council (no voting rights)
- Submits reports to the European Parliament

qm: qualified majority

Rotating Presidency to be abolished

Council is to represent the EU externally without encroaching on the role of the President of the Commission and the → Union's Minister for Foreign Affairs.

A vague division of tasks

However, the division of tasks between the President of the European Council and the Minister for Foreign Affairs in the Constitution is rather vague. Only experience will show whether these two individuals can work effectively together. The main institutional task of the new President of the European Council will be to provide the EU with greater continuity. But equally important, given public apathy, will be providing the European electorate with a public face through whom they can channel their approval or disapproval of the European Council's policies.

7.4 The Council of Ministers

In the Council of Ministers (often referred to as the "Council of the European Union" or simply as the "Council"), the governments of the EU countries are each represented by one person at the ministerial level. Until now, the chair in the Council of Ministers has rotated once every six months. The country which has the chair is referred to as the Presidency of the Council.

Meetings of the portfolio ministers

The Council of Ministers meets in different configurations, which are determined by the topic being discussed—ministers for finance attend the "Economic and Financial Affairs Council" and foreign ministers meet to discuss international affairs.

The Council of Ministers is responsible for legislation in conjunction with the European Parliament, for the coordination of economic policy within the EU, for drawing up the budgetary plan together with the EP, for the Common Foreign and Security Policy, and for the coordination of the member states in police and judicial cooperation.

Depending on the policy area, decisions are made unanimously, or on the basis of a simple or qualified majority. In the case of a qualified majority, the Treaty of Nice stipulates a weighting of the votes. Depending on the size of the population, the member states have between 3 (Luxembourg) and 29 votes (Germany, France, the United Kingdom, Italy). In the EU 27, the qualified majority amounts to 255 out of a total of 345 votes (73.9 percent).

The Council of Ministers of the European Union

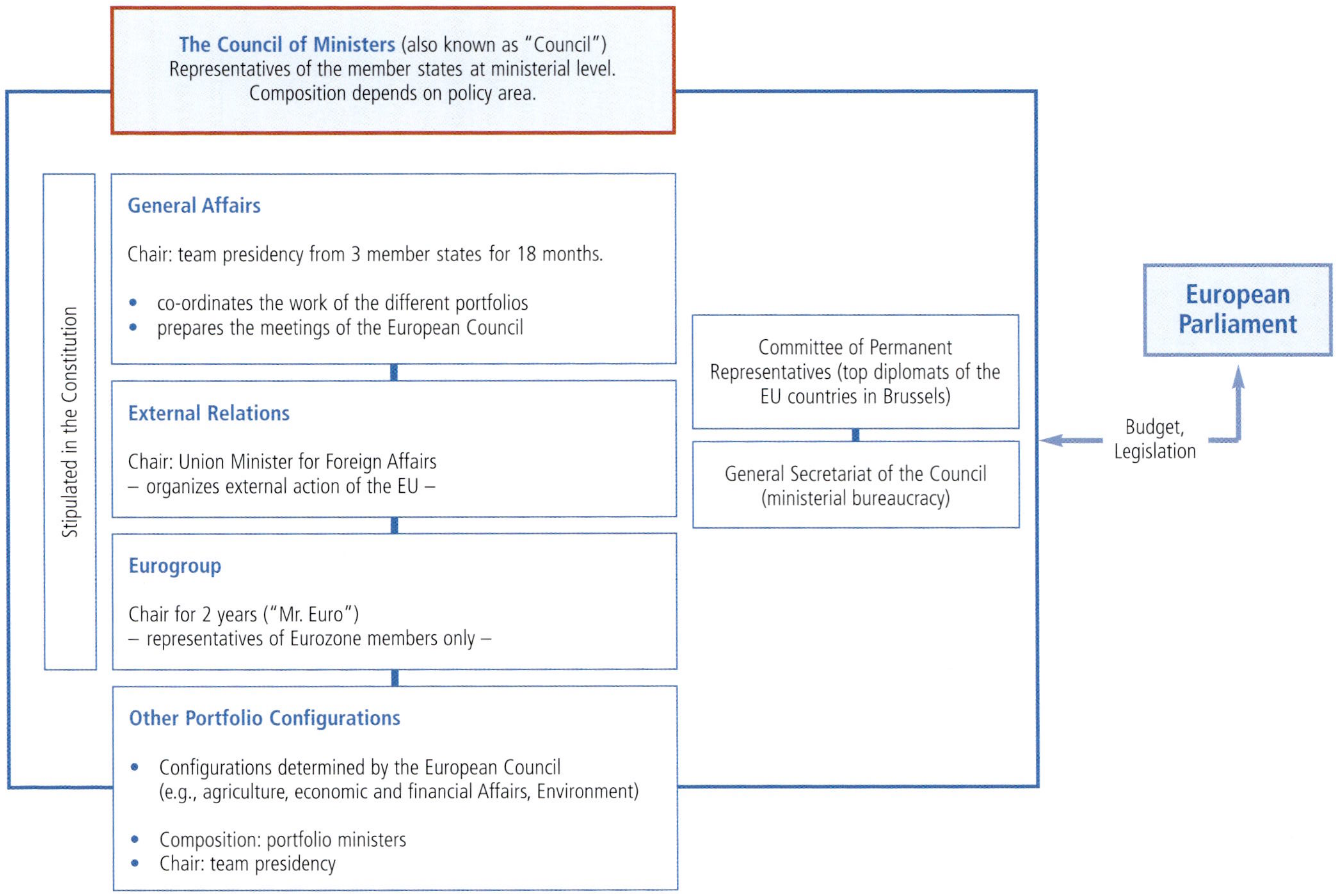

What changes does the Constitution introduce with regard to the Council of Ministers?

In the future, the "General Affairs Council" will have the task of ensuring that the work of the Council of Ministers in its various guises becomes more effective. The body's brief is to prepare for the meetings of the Heads of State and Government in conjunction with the President of the European Council and the Commission. The Constitution also makes provision for a "Foreign Affairs Council" chaired by the new → Union's Minister for Foreign Affairs.

The European Council can sanction other configurations of the Council of Ministers (see diagram, p. 69) on the basis of a "European decision." A range of the various Council configurations will probably continue to exist for the foreseeable future. Thus, there will probably be, for instance, a Council configuration for Agriculture and Fisheries, one for Justice and Home Affairs, and one for Economic and Financial Affairs.

Independent body: the Euro Group

The Constitution upgrades the "Euro Group" to become an institutional body in its own right—a move that is long overdue. The group of the countries in the euro zone elects its chairman, informally known as "Mr. or Mrs. Euro," for a period of two-and-a-half years. Although the Constitution has not entered into force, the first President of the Euro Group, Luxembourg Prime Minister Jean-Claude Juncker, was elected in September 2004. The new body of euro zone countries will be strengthened by the fact that it can, in the future, make more decisions on its own without reference to the other EU countries.

Council of Ministers to meet in public

The Constitution also states that the Council of Ministers is to meet in public when it deliberates and votes on legislative proposals. One proposal missing from the Constitution is the creation of a separate Legislative Council in which the adoption of all legislative acts could be coordinated and synchronized. Such a body could prevent the individual decisions of various Council configurations from contradicting each other.

Team presidencies for 18 months

The Constitution transforms the leadership of the Council of Ministers. Since the traditional semi-annual rotation of the chair is no longer feasible in a European Union with over 27 member states, the Constitution envisages the introduction of team presidencies (three states) for a duration of 18 months, in which one of the member states has the chair for six months in all of the portfolio councils. However, there is a risk that the countries taking part in a team presidency might become competitors.

Important innovations

Two other reforms introduced by the Constitution will radically change the function of the Council of Ministers. The number of cases in which the Council can make a decision on the basis of a → qualified majority (see Chapter 8.1) will be increased. The current triple majority decision-making procedure adopted in Nice will be abolished and replaced with the → double majority (55 percent of the member states—at least 15—representing 65 percent of the population of the EU).

The new voting procedure reduces the possibility of deadlock in the Council of Ministers.

7.5 The European Commission

The Commission: the "engine" of the EU

The European Commission is considered to be the "engine" of the EU. In the EU of 27 members, it consists of 26 commissioners nominated by the EU countries and a President who is appointed by the Heads of State and Government. The European Parliament is required to give its consent to his or her appointment. Every member state is represented in the Commission.

The Commission's tasks

The Commission is designed to be a supranational independent authority. It can initiate legislation and ensure that legislation is implemented in its capacity as an executive body; take new initiatives to promote EU interests; and oversee the compliance of member states with the European Treaties ("watchdog of the Treaties"). It is also the negotiating partner for the accession candidates, it executes the budget plan and is in charge of the EU's programming.

What changes does the Constitution introduce with regard to the European Commission?

The Constitution does not change the tasks the European Commission is required to perform. In the medium term, the Com-

The European Commission

The European Commission

Composition and Organization

- One commissioner per country until 2014
- After 2014 to be reduced to two-thirds of the Member States (e.g., 27 states, 18 commissioners)
- Commission is appointed by the European Council after receiving consent of the European Parliament
- Term of office: 5 years

President

Nominated (qm) by the European Council, which takes into account the elections to the European Parliament. The President's tasks include

- to lay down guidelines
- to decide on the internal organization of the Commission

Vice-Presidents

- Appointed by the President of the Commission.

Exception:
The Union Minister for Foreign Affairs

Commissioners

- Nominated by the Member States in conjunction with the President of the Commission
- Member States on equal footing after the reduction in 2014

Tasks of the Commission

- Monopoly on initiating legislation
- to initiate annual/multi-annual programming
- to oversee the application of EU law
- to execute budget plan
- External representation (exception: CFSP)

qm: qualified majority
CFSP: Common Foreign and Security Policy

mission will profit from the fact that the powers of its President have been expanded and are more clearly defined. This improves the position of the President vis-à-vis the college of commissioners, and ensures that he or she has the ability to make decisions even in the case of insurmountable differences with individual commissioners.

Stronger Commission President

From the Commission's point of view it is a positive fact that (in so far as the document does not explicitly state otherwise) legislative acts can be initiated only at the suggestion of the Commission ("right of initiative").

Right of initiative

From 2014 onwards, the Commission will be leaner. The number of its members will then correspond to two-thirds of the number of member states. If there are 27 or 28 member states, there will be 18 commissioners. States will be able to nominate commissioners in rotation for a uniform period in office.

A smaller Commission

The reduction in its size will allow the Commission to function even if there is further enlargement. Otherwise, it would be virtually impossible for a variety of reasons to cope with a situation in which every country in an EU with 28 or more states could send a commissioner to Brussels. First, every member of the Commission is supposed to be given a meaningful task, which will prove highly difficult in a college with 27 or more commissioners. Secondly, the commissioners' responsibilities should not overlap. Thirdly, the commission should be small enough to allow commissioners to deliberate together.

The reduction in the size of the Commission has been a controversial issue for years. Small countries are especially keen on having their own commissioner, whom they see as a guardian of their interests. Afraid of losing their influence in Brussels, they see their commissioner as an important mediator between the EU and their citizens.

Constitution strengthens Commission

Overall, the Constitutional Treaty strengthens the position of the EU Commission and its President in the new institutional architecture of the European Union (see diagrams on p. 62 and p. 72). However, it cannot be assumed that the reforms enshrined in the Constitution will be sufficient to strengthen the strategic position of the Commission within the EU's structure—a position which has been weakened in recent years. The Commission's power to get things done will depend in the future on whether it is considered primarily an administrative body, as the "bureaucratic authority in Brussels," or whether it will succeed in shaping the EU's political agenda.

7.6 The Union Minister for Foreign Affairs

New: the Union Minister for Foreign Affairs

The creation of a Minister for Foreign Affairs is another important alteration in the institutional structure of the EU (see diagram, p. 75). In the future, the office of the Commissioner for Foreign Affairs (currently held by Benita Ferrero-Waldner, the Austrian Commissioner) and that of the High Representative for the Common Foreign and Security Policy (currently the Spaniard Javier Solana) are to be combined.

Two functions in two institutions

The Union Minister for Foreign Affairs is elected through qualified majority by the European Council and with the consent of the President of the Commission for a period of five years. He or she is also one of the Vice-Presidents of the European Commission. Furthermore, he or she chairs the "Foreign Affairs Council" and thus in one person combines two functions in two institutions, the Commission and the Council.

EU foreign policy profile strengthened

The Union's Minister for Foreign Affairs will conduct the Common Foreign and Security Policy of the Union, ensure that the decisions made by the European Council and the Council of Ministers are implemented, and represent the EU in international organizations (UN Security Council, etc.). In addition to this he or she will have a right of initiative in the areas of foreign, security and defense policy. This means that the Union Minister for Foreign Affairs will possess functions that go far beyond those of the High Representative or the Commissioner for Foreign Relations. This will strengthen the foreign policy profile of the EU.

Danger of disputed competences

However, the "double hat" arrangement may also turn out to be problematic. In the future, there could be disputes between the EU Minister for Foreign Affairs and the President of the European Council, who, in turn, could clash with the President of the Commission. The ambiguous role of the Union Minister for Foreign Affairs could also be detrimental to the Commission, which might be held accountable for decisions for which the (European) Council bears the political responsibility.

The Union Minister for Foreign Affairs

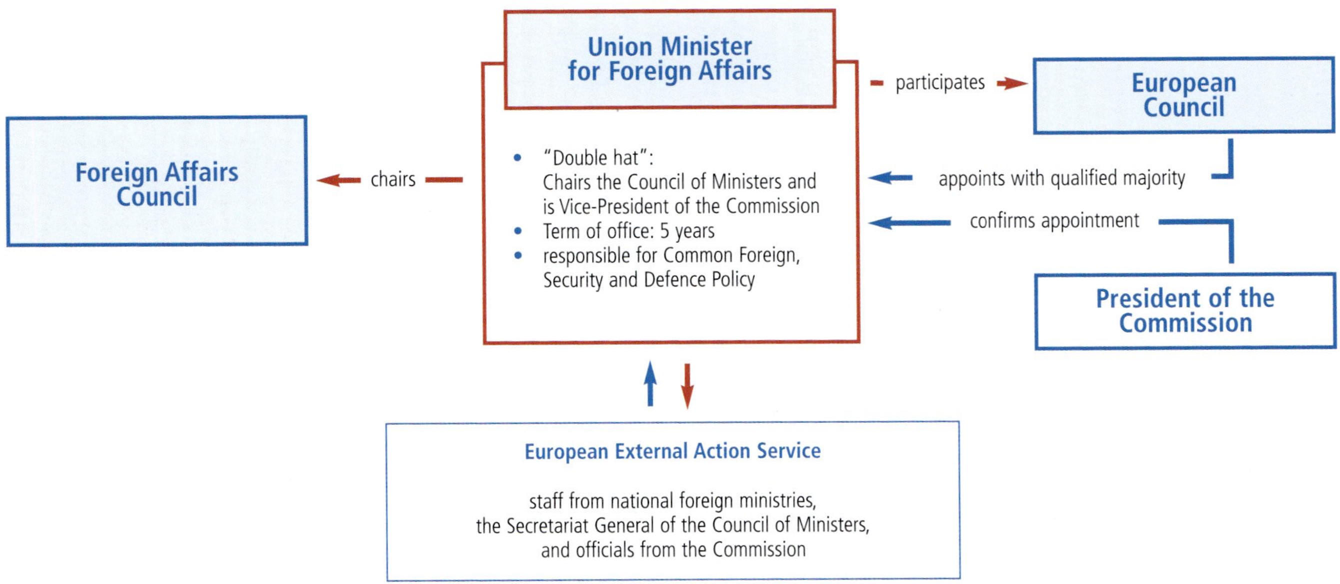

7.7 The European External Action Service

Union Minister for Foreign Affairs has his or her own diplomats

In order to be able to perform a wide range of tasks, the Union Minister for Foreign Affairs will receive considerable administrative support. In addition to the 120 EU delegations all over the world that are to be placed under his or her control, the Union Minister for Foreign Affairs will be supported by the newly established European External Action Service (EAS).

The EAS is made up of officials from the General Secretariat of the Council of Ministers, the Commission and seconded members of national diplomatic services. The new service will promote a dialogue between the institutions and the diplomats, encourage the establishment of a common culture of foreign policy attitudes and improve the representation of the EU vis-à-vis non-EU states. The preparations for the establishment of the service have already begun, even though the Constitution is not yet in force.

Putting a face on the EU

Policies that are to be comprehensible to the public must have a public face. Until now, this has very rarely been the case in the European Union. The Constitution will create high profile figures in the new Union Minister for Foreign Affairs, the President of the European Council and the strengthened President of the Commission. In the future, the citizens of Europe will be familiar with the incumbents of these offices. They will be the focal points of trust and distrust, agreement and disagreement. This personalization will help to overcome the EU's difficulty in connecting with Europe's electorate.

8 Decision-making processes in the EU Constitution

If the EU is to take decisive action, decision-making and voting procedures in the Council of Ministers and in the European Parliament will have to be reformed, and the parliaments and citizens of the member states must be encouraged to play a greater role. The Constitution contains innovations such as the introduction of double majority, the extension of majority decisions, and the introduction of citizens' initiatives.

Reform of the decision-making and voting procedures

8.1 Double majority

Double majority: a milestone in EU history

One of the most important innovations of the European Constitution is the introduction of a new voting procedure in the Council of Ministers, which legislates in conjunction with the European Parliament. According to the Treaty of Nice currently in force, a qualified majority can materialize only if it comprises the majority of the weighted votes, more than half of the EU states, and at least 62 percent of the EU population ("triple majority").

The Constitutional Treaty abolishes the complicated weighting of votes and stipulates that from November 1, 2009 onwards, qualified majorities in the Council must comprise the majority of the member states (55 percent, the so-called "states quorum") and the majority of the EU population (65 percent, the "population quorum"). If the decision is not based on an initiative from the Commission or the Union Minister for Foreign Affairs, the required majority actually increases to 72 percent of the member states, which must represent at least 65 percent of the EU population.

Preventing blocking coalitions

The introduction of the double majority is a milestone in the development of the European Union. On the one hand, the new voting procedure reflects the nature of the EU as a union of states and citizens. On the other hand, it makes it easier to reach decisions, since it encourages the formation of majorities and reduces the number of blocking coalitions in the Council of Ministers.

New balance of power

The introduction of the double majority changes the weight of the various countries in the Council of Ministers. Criticism came at an early stage, primarily from Poland and Spain, which feared that, with the double majority system, they would lose their influence in comparison with the largest states. Although in absolute terms both countries are even slightly better off as a result of the new voting procedure, there is some truth in their complaint that they will lose influence when compared to the most populous states—Germany, France, the United Kingdom and Italy. In relative terms, Germany will obtain the greatest increase in power as a result of the double majority rule.

8.2 The extension of majority decisions

Danger of decision-making deadlock

Until now, the work of the Council of Ministers has been impeded by the fact that in many cases it has required unanimity. This leads to decision-making deadlock and lowest common denominator decisions.

Constitution facilitates faster decision-making

In the Constitution the number of cases in which the Council decides on the basis of a qualified majority has been extended from 137 to 181. In certain areas, such as asylum and immigration policy or border controls, this will lead to faster and better decisions.

However, there are still 70 areas in which the Council has to decide unanimously. These include critical areas such as taxes, social security, the establishment of the multi-annual financial framework, and virtually the whole area of the Common Foreign and Security Policy. Following strong pressure from Britain (and low tax countries in Eastern Europe such as Slovakia), plans to harmonize corporate tax by majority vote were overruled. National vetoes were maintained over tax, foreign policy and social security, and the EU budget.

Bridging clause

The Constitution contains a method with which it effects a gradual reduction in the use of the right of veto. This makes it possible to improve decision-making processes without a complicated → intergovernmental conference in those areas in which the resistance of certain member states has prevented a transition to qualified majority decisions (→ bridging clause). Thus the European Council can empower the Council of Ministers to vote in a certain area on the basis of a qualified majority.

In theory, the new regulations reinforce the ability of the EU to continue to develop dynamically with regard to the use of majority decision-making in the Council of Ministers. However, it is unclear to what extent this procedure will be used in practice, since such constitutional developments would require a unanimous decision by the Heads of State and Government.

8.3 The co-decision procedure in the "ordinary legislative procedure"

EP: greater legislative importance

The co-decision procedure is the European Parliament's strongest instrument of power, for here it participates in legislation on an equal footing with the Council of Ministers. However, this procedure has not previously been applied in every case. The EU Constitution would change this state of affairs, since it elevates the co-decision procedure in conjunction with the → double majority in the Council of Ministers to the status of the "ordinary legislative procedure" (see diagram, p. 80).

At the same time, the areas in which the co-decision procedure is to be applied have been extended. This enhances the significance of the Parliament in the legislative process.

Constitution simplifies legislation

Furthermore, the EU's legislative procedure will be simplified by the fact that what is known as the "ordinary legislative procedure" (the co-decision procedure in conjunction with qualified majority) is to be the normal legislative procedure. It envisages that both the European Parliament and the Council must give their consent to legislation proposed by the European Commission. If the Council and the Parliament fail to reach agreement, there will be a conciliation procedure.

Only in certain specific cases will it be possible to deviate from customary legislative procedure. Special kinds of legislative procedure make it possible for the Council acting alone to adopt legis-

Ordinary legislative procedure

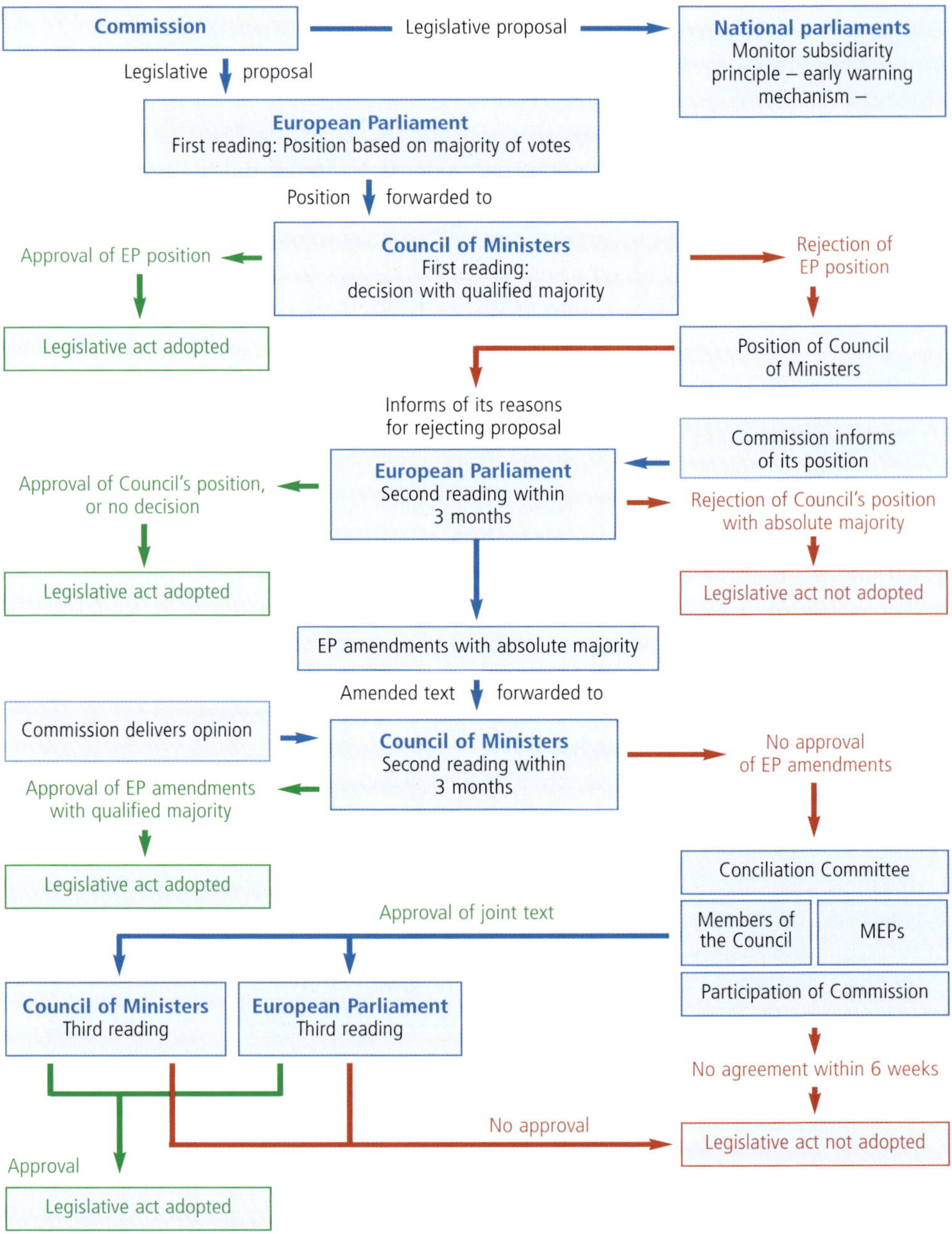

lation with weaker participatory rights for the European Parliament.

8.4 Decrease in the number of legal instruments and terminological simplification

Fewer legal instruments

The provisions relating to the legal instruments available to the EU have been considerably simplified in the Constitutional Treaty. The number of instruments has been reduced significantly (see diagram, p. 82). In the current Treaties there are 15 different instruments. Apart from the most important—the regulation and the directive—these are, for example, decisions, general principles and guidelines, common strategies, common positions and joint actions. It is not clear how to distinguish between these terms—they are not particularly meaningful.

The Constitutional Treaty reduces the number of legal instruments to six: European law, European framework law, regulation, decision, recommendation, and opinion. Laws can be adopted either in the form of European legislation or European framework legislation.

European laws and framework laws

European laws correspond to what have been previously known as "regulations" and are directly enforceable in all EU countries. European framework laws (previously known as directives) merely supply, as the name indicates, a framework and require implementation through national legislation.

In the Constitution, legislative acts without the character of a law are called "European decisions" and "European regulations." In addition to this, there are also the special categories "delegated European regulation," "European implementing regulation," and "European implementing decision," with which the European Commission or the Council can introduce uniform, law-based implementing measures. Recommendations and opinions are acts that are not legally binding.

The legal instruments of the European Union

Current legal situation (Treaty of Nice):
More than 15 legal instruments

- Regulation
- Agreement (EC Treaty)
- Agreement (EU Treaty)

- Directive
- Framework directive
- Decision

- Decision (Title V EU Treaty)
- Decision (Title VI EC Treaty)
- General principles and guidelines
- Common strategy
- Joint action

- Common position (Title V EC Treaty)
- Common position (Title VI EU Treaty)
- Recommendation

- Opinion

New legal situation (European Constitution):
Six legal instruments

- **European law** – binding general legislation, directly applicable in all member states (formerly known as regulation).
- **European framework law** – legislation binding on member states. They can choose in which form they need to implement it (formerly known as directives).
- **European regulation** – non-legislative act that implements certain provisions of the Constitution.
- **European decision** – a binding non-legislative act. If it specifies to those whom it is addressed it is binding only on them.
- **Recommendations of EU institutions** – have no binding force.
- **Opinions of EU institutions** – have no binding force.

8.5 Early warning mechanism: more rights for the national parliaments

The Constitutional Treaty confers greater rights on the national parliaments to object if the Commission proposes to introduce EU regulations in an area that can be dealt with just as well or better at a national, regional or local level. With the introduction of what is known as the "early warning mechanism," national parliaments will be able to protest within a period of six weeks against a legislative proposal by the European Commission if they believe it infringes the principles of → subsidiarity or proportionality. If one third of national parliaments object to an EU law, the Commission must reconsider it.

In the procedure every parliament has two votes. For Britain this means that the House of Commons and the House of Lords each have one vote, in Germany the votes are divided between the Bundestag and the Bundesrat. If at least a third of the votes from the national parliaments submit "justified opinions" on an EU proposal, the Commission is required to re-examine its proposals and subsequently to justify what it proposes to do next.

More rights for national Parliaments

Early warning mechanism

Legislative proposals by the Commission are sent to national parliament and, if necessary, regional parliaments (e.g., the German States, "Bundesländer") would be consulted.

The mechanism enhances the rights of national parliaments that for the first time are now integrated into decision-making across the EU level. There will be a period of six weeks in which to submit opinions (statements explaining why the proposals breach the principle of subsidiarity).

The appeal is sent to the Presidents of the European Parliament, the Council, and the Commission. The Commission is obliged to re-examine the legislative proposal if a critical mass of the Parliaments holds that it breaches the principle of subsidiarity.

Appeal to the European Court of Justice is possible

This allows national parliaments to show the European Commission the "yellow card." Member states, after the entry into force of EU legislation, may lodge an appeal with the European Court of Justice if they think that the → principle of subsidiarity has been infringed. The second vote also strengthens the House of Lords or the Bundesrat, which partly compensates for the threat to its competences.

8.6 Citizens' initiative

Direct citizen participation

The Constitution envisages the introduction of citizens' initiatives. This means that citizens will, for the very first time, be able to participate directly in European politics. The precondition for the implementation of a citizens' initiative is that if a million citizens (only 0.2 percent of the EU population) from a "significant" number of member states demand legislation with their signatures, the Commission must act and submit a proposal. However, the Constitution remains vague about the requisite number of countries.

8.7 The Constitutional Treaty creates greater opportunities for a "Europe of different speeds"

In an EU of 27+, the differences between the interests of the various countries will become greater, and ideas about the future of the Union will diverge ever more strongly. The simultaneous attainment of steps towards integration in all the member states will become increasingly difficult.

Differentiated integration

In the past, in the case of monetary (euro), internal (Schengen) or social policies (introduction of minimum standards), deadlock was overcome through "differentiated integration." It proved possible to promote the integration process in this way in the past. Differentiated integration means that not every EU country has to join in every project from the start, but that smaller groups can forge ahead in a specific policy area.

In order to promote the future development of the European Union, it will be even more necessary than in the past for various

Various forms of differentiated integration

Enhanced co-operation

The Constitution has refined the principal instrument of differentiation within the EU. Enhanced co-operation may be used only as a "last resort" if a proposal cannot be implemented involving the participation of all EU countries within a "reasonable period". The Constitution stipulates that at least a third of the member states must take part in enhanced co-operation.

Permanent structured co-operation

According to the Constitution, member states that fulfill "higher criteria" in their military capabilities can establish permanent structured (military) co-operation.

Missions on behalf of the EU

Member states that possess the necessary capabilities and wish to participate can take on EU missions.

Co-operation in the Defence Agency

EU member states can form different groups within the newly established European Defence Agency and implement common defence projects.

Constructive abstention

Every EU state can abstain from certain votes relating to the Common Foreign and Security Policy in the Council of Ministers. In such cases the member state in question is not required to implement the decision, though it accepts that the decision adopted by the other member states is binding for the EU as a whole.

Euro Group

The Constitution enhances the possibility of pursuing independent economic policy within the Eurozone, and strengthens the external representation of the Euro Group. For the first time, the Euro Group is recognized as a body in its own right in a protocol appended to the Constitution. The Euro Group is permitted to elect its chair for a period of two-and-a-half years.

Withdrawal clause

"External differentiation" is now possible as a result of the new withdrawal clause. Whereas flexibility has previously been used to accelerate internal integration, the withdrawal clause gives countries the flexibility to head in the opposite direction.

groups of countries to cooperate more closely in certain policy areas. However, there is a danger of the long-term exclusion of other countries, and the possibility that integration will begin to fray at the edges.

New and improved instruments

The Constitutional Treaty contains a whole series of new and improved instruments of differentiation (see diagram above). They include the revised version of the existing instrument of "enhanced cooperation" and the introduction of new differentiation instruments in foreign, security and defense policy.

Revised version of enhanced cooperation

"Enhanced cooperation" is the central instrument of differentiation in the European Treaties. It was introduced in Amsterdam and amended in Nice. Without mentioning any specific areas of application, the provisions relating to enhanced cooperation list conditions under which a group of EU countries can work together more closely.

The provisions are designed to ensure that such cooperation does not contradict the goals of the European Treaties or exclude other member states in the long term. This instrument has never been used in practice. The catalogue of conditions had the effect of a straitjacket, and the EU countries have not yet had enough political will to apply the instrument of enhanced cooperation in practice.

Clear and practical provisions

In the Constitutional Treaty the legal provisions governing enhanced cooperation are bundled and simplified. The instrument is decoupled from certain restrictive requirements, and more clear provisions are defined for applying the instrument in practice. Furthermore, in contrast to the Nice Treaty, the Constitutional Treaty allows for the application of enhanced cooperation in the entire area of foreign, security and defense policy.

A third of the EU member states must participate

The Constitution stipulates that at least a third of the member states must participate in an enhanced cooperation. Thus, a "critical mass" of participating states has to be reached. Enhanced cooperation may be used only as "a last resort" if a certain objective or goal cannot be attained with the participation of all EU countries within a "reasonable period."

To further the objectives of the Union

The rights of the non-participating member states must be respected. The internal market, economic cohesion and trade must not be undermined, nor is it permissible to distort competition. Enhanced cooperation must aim to further the objectives of the Union, protect its interests and reinforce its integration process. Both at its inception and subsequently, it must be open to all the member states. The later participation of a country may be linked to certain conditions.

New instruments of differentiation in the area of security and defense policy

The majority of specific ideas for greater differentiation are mooted in security and defense policy. The current Treaty of Nice does not envisage differentiated integration for this policy area. The Constitutional Treaty changes this.

In addition to the instrument of enhanced cooperation, which in the future will also apply to the European Security and Defence Policy (ESDP), the Constitution contains a number of special forms of differentiated cooperation for this policy area.

The new instruments pay tribute to the fact that the different security policy traditions of the member states, the increasingly heterogeneous nature of their interests, the different strengths and capabilities of their national armed forces and the budgetary and economic policy dissimilarities between the members of an EU 27+ require a higher degree of differentiation.

The new differentiation instruments in the ESDP include (1) → "permanent structured cooperation," (2) the assignment of EU missions to a group of member states, and (3) cooperation of individual EU countries within the framework of the new European Defence Agency.

1. Permanent structured (military) cooperation

The Constitutional Treaty envisages that those countries which fulfill "higher criteria" in their military capabilities and which, with regard to the most demanding missions, "have made more binding commitments to one another," can establish permanent structured cooperation within the Union framework.

The preconditions for participation in permanent structured cooperation and a series of specific implementing measures are contained in a protocol appended to the Constitution.

Permanent structured cooperation, in contrast to the general method of differentiation proffered by enhanced cooperation (the practical use of which must still be decided in practice) is already a first step towards a European security and defense union within the EU in which not all countries have to participate from the start.

States can preserve their military neutrality

Thus, after Schengen and after the introduction of the euro, one of the principal future integration projects may perhaps begin with the help of differentiated integration. States such as Finland or Austria are thus given the opportunity to preserve their neutral status with regard to military matters.

2. Cooperation in the Defence Agency

Increasing military capabilities

The Constitutional Treaty proposes the establishment of a European Defence Agency for defense capabilities development, research, acquisition and armaments. Its purpose is to improve the EU's strategic, operational and technological capabilities. States may form various groups within the Agency and implement joint projects. This form of cooperation can make a contribution to the more efficient use of defense budgets and ensure the incorporation of all the member states in the EU's overall defense policy strategy, regardless of the size of their armed forces or the resources of their armaments industries.

3. Missions in the name of the European Union

In the future, member states which possess the necessary capabilities and wish to participate can be commissioned to carry out an EU mission. A group of countries—a minimum number is not stipulated—may carry out missions involving disarmament operations, rescue missions, conflict prevention, peace-keeping and peace-making measures, and post-conflict stabilization operations.

Missions under the EU flag

This form of differentiation makes it possible to embed a "coalition of the willing" in the structures and the legal framework of the European Union. Countries which are prepared to become more involved in civil or military crisis management can act under the flag of the EU, thereby increasing their political legitimacy.

On the other hand, states not participating in the mission can still influence their EU partners. They would not have this opportunity if the participating EU countries were to organize themselves outside the European Union.

9 The process of ratifying the EU Constitution

9.1 The current state of the ratification process

Fate of the constitution uncertain

"The Constitution must be ratified now," said Joschka Fischer, former German Minister for Foreign Affairs, in 2004. "There will be some fuss, but in the end it will enter into force." More than two years after the Constitution was signed, Fischer's optimistic prediction has been disproved.

Requiring the ratification of all 27 member states, the bar for the European Constitution's success was always set high, which was probably underestimated by commentators at the time. Initially, 15 countries planned to use Parliament to decide the issue, whilst ten countries planned to consult the electorate through referenda.

Two founding states say "no"

The ratification process got off to a successful start when parliaments in Lithuania, Hungary, Slovenia, Italy, Greece and Slovakia ratified the European Constitution until mid May 2005. The same month, Spain voted in favor of the Constitution in the first popular referendum with a large majority, and parliaments in Austria and Germany ratified the text. Bulgaria and Romania ratified the Constitution in the framework of their accession treaties. However, during a single momentous week in May and June 2005, the French voted "non" and the Dutch voted "nee," throwing the European Union into turmoil. Though referenda had been lost on the EU before (Ireland famously voted against the Nice Treaty), this was the first time that two founders of the European Union had decisively rejected a new European treaty. The internal debates in these countries during the referendum campaigns are worth a closer look:

The constitutional debate in France

In France, the Constitution was presented by the "no" camp as a vehicle for neoliberal economics and immigration. There was frequent talk of competition from Polish plumbers and a hemorrhaging of jobs to the east—"délocalisation" in the popular phrase. French language and culture were described as under siege through globalization—a process that the free-market European Commission was seen as championing. Fears that control of the EU was being lost to the new liberal states in the east were exacerbated by the prospect of Turkey entering into the EU. This proved a powerful argument for the anti-Constitution campaign, since, according to polls, Turkish entry into the EU is opposed by more than half of French voters.

In truth, however, the long Constitution document was blamed for a bewildering array of contradictory ills. Socialists accused the text of being "liberal"; French President Jacques Chirac said that it was "social." Voters were left unsure and therefore felt safest casting a "no" vote. Yet it would be wrong to argue that voters were apathetic about the issues being discussed. Eighty-three percent of French voters stated that they had discussed the Constitution with their friends and family. Over nine million tuned in to watch the leading socialist "no" campaigner Laurent Fabius—a larger audience than that for the French Cup final.

In the end, dissatisfaction with France's political elite—particularly with President Jacques Chirac and the Government of Jean-Pierre Raffarin—, following years of slow growth and high unemployment, had a huge impact. All mainstream parties—from Chirac's ruling Union pour un Mouvement Populaire (UMP) to the Socialist party on the left—were officially in favor of a "yes" vote. But for the first time, there were splits on the left. A Socialist "no" Group condemned the Constitution as the unacceptable expression of "free and unbridled competition" and campaigned under the slogan "A different Constitution for a different Europe."

The Dutch debate

In the Netherlands, where a huge 62 percent of voters opposed the Constitution, the same urge to give the political elite a bloody nose led to the "nee" vote. Voters were particularly angered by pro-European politicians predicting economic collapse if the Constitutional Treaty was rejected and describing anti-Constitution sentiment as uninformed ignorance.

In the aftermath of the failed referenda in France and the Netherlands, states such as the Czech Republic, Denmark, Ireland, Poland, Portugal, Sweden and the UK decided to postpone ratification. In Britain, Tony Blair had originally opposed the idea of a European Constitution, echoing the virulent opposition from Britain's tabloid press and claimed to see "no case for having a referendum on an EU Constitution." Eventually, when the Constitution seemed like a foregone conclusion, Britain shifted its ground to nervous and grudging support. The government tried to downplay the importance of the EU Constitution with the then Europe Minister Peter Hain describing it as a "tidying-up exercise" of little importance. With public opinion becoming increasingly hostile towards the EU, it was understandable that Blair was nervous about putting the Constitution to a public vote. Yet, with newspapers and opposition parties in full cry, Blair gave in to the pressure. After all, those demanding a referendum had a strong case. In Britain, referenda had been widely used since 1997. However, Blair would have had to pull off the biggest political success of his career by transforming 2:1 public opposition to the Constitution into a victory. Most commentators felt that this task was impossible. In the end, Blair's political luck held. It was with barely disguised relief that he was able to call off the popular vote in the face of the Dutch and French results.

Ratification postponed in several member states

However, other member states continued the ratification process. Parliaments in Latvia, Cyprus and Malta ratified the Constitution in summer 2005. Luxemburg even held a successful referendum in July 2005. Belgium, Estonia and Finland then ratified the Constitution in 2006. At the time of this writing (February 2007), 18 member states, which constitute over 50 percent of the population of the EU, have ratified the European Constitution. Still, this hardly solves the problem, since the introduction into force of the Constitutional Treaty requires ratification by all member states.

More than half of the EU electorate has already ratified the Treaty

9.2 Overcoming the ratification crisis

Since the scale of the "no" votes became clear, EU leaders have been divided about how they should proceed. In the immediate aftermath of the votes in summer 2005, it was agreed that there should be a year's "period of reflection" before deciding on a plan. The Austrian EU Presidency in the first half of 2006 tried to revive the Constitution, declaring that it was "not dead," but simply "not in force." Eventually, though, after consulting with other leaders, the Austrian Foreign Minister concluded that "this issue cannot be settled satisfactorily and conclusively for all 27 member states at this present time." Yet again, in the absence of any solution, the project "Constitution" was resumed. Now it will be up to Chancellor Angela Merkel and the German EU Presidency in the first half of 2007 to set the course regarding the constitutional basis of the EU.

An instrument inserted in the Constitution text declared that if, two years after Rome, four-fifths of the countries had ratified the Constitution, but some had "encountered difficulties," an EU summit would be held to consider the situation. The plan held that once 80 percent of member states had ratified the Constitution, the European Council should meet to decide what to do with those who cannot ratify.

Alternatives to implementing the Constitution

There is no simple route through this institutional stalemate. One option is to retain the Treaty of Nice currently in force. But this is to all intents and purposes not a viable option. The EU of 27 member states cannot be governed on the basis of a set of rules and regulations that in essence was originally conceived for six states. Without meaningful amendments to the Treaty of Nice, the European Union will sooner or later experience a dramatic crisis of legitimacy. The option of holding on to the original Constitutional Treaty presupposes that the new primary law will be presented unaltered to the French and Dutch electorates in another referendum. However, the chances that a second referendum will lead to the desired result seem rather slim. The option of making the most of Nice is not sufficient to ensure the enlarged EU's future efficiency or to enhance its democratic legitimacy. The implementation of constitutional innovations on the basis of the existing Treaties and thus beneath the level of formal amendments to primary law is unlikely to be achieved in many important cases. Attempts to unravel the package as a whole and to "cherry-pick" individual elements of the Constitutional Treaty will come up against opposition from certain member states and thus fail.

A pragmatic option would be to transfer the core of the constitutional innovations into primary law in the shape of a treaty amending the Treaty of Nice. The Bertelsmann Stiftung and the Center for Applied Policy Research (CAP) have suggested a possible means of doing this: The "Treaty Amending the Treaty of Nice" is a less comprehensive treaty which, around 50 pages in length, contains only about a tenth of the text in the present Constitution. It includes the following constitutional innovations:

Treaty Amending the Treaty of Nice

(1) the reform of the EU's institutional system,
(2) the development of the decision-making and voting procedures,
(3) the reform and enhancement of the instruments of differentiated integration and
(4) other constitutional innovations.

(1) Reform of the institutional system

The Constitution's central institutional reforms should be incorporated into the current Treaties. They primarily comprise the appointment of an elected President of the European Council, the introduction of a Union Minister for Foreign Affairs, and the reduction in the size of the European Commission and the strengthening of its President. The personalization of the architecture of European leadership makes it possible to achieve a clear assignment of responsibilities on the EU level and strengthens the continuity, visibility and consistency of European policymaking.

(2) The development of the decision-making and voting procedures

If the EU wishes to keep its ability to take action and to enhance its democratic legitimacy, it needs to reform the decision-making procedures in the Council of Ministers and the European Parliament, and assign a more prominent role to the national parliaments. The introduction of the double majority procedure constitutes a milestone in the history of the European Union. Using the number of citizens and the number of states as a basis for decision-making in the Council of Ministers reflects the two strands of legitimacy in the EU. The double majority rule makes

Ratification of the Constitution in the

Member State	Ratification Procedure[1)]	Date[2)]	Status
Austria	parliamentary (both chambers)	11 May 2005 and 25 May 2005	ratified
Belgium	parliamentary (both chambers + regional parliaments)	8 February 2006	ratified
Bulgaria	parliamentary ratification of the accession treaty	11 May 2005	ratified
Cyprus	optional referendum	30 June 2005	ratified
Czech Republic	parliamentary	not yet available	open
Denmark	obligatory referendum	not yet available[3)]	open
Estonia	parliamentary	9 May 2006	ratified
Finland	parliamentary	5 December 2006	ratified
France	optional referendum	29 May 2005	failure
Germany	parliamentary (both chambers)	12 May 2005 and 27 May 2005	ratified
Greece	parliamentary	19 April 2005	ratified
Hungary	parliamentary	20 December 2004	ratified
Ireland	obligatory referendum + parliamentary	not yet available[3)]	open
Italy	parliamentary (both chambers)	25 January 2005 and 6 April 2005	ratified

[1)] There are different constitutional stipulations regulating the ratification of international treaties in the various member states.

Parliamentary: National parliaments adopt the Treaty establishing a Constitution for Europe by means of legislation pertaining to ratification.

Plebiscitary by means of an obligatory or voluntary referendum: The electorate is asked to vote for or against the constitutional text in a referendum. Only Denmark and Ireland intend to hold an obligatory referendum

27 member states of the European Union

Member state	Ratification procedure[1)]	Date[2)]	Status
Latvia	parliamentary	2 June 2005	ratified
Lithuania	parliamentary	11 November 2004	ratified
Luxembourg	consultative referendum + parliamentary	10 July 2005	ratified
Malta	parliamentary	6 July 2005	ratified
Netherlands	consultative referendum + parliamentary (both chambers)	1 June 2005 (referendum)	open
Poland	probably optional referendum	not yet available[3)]	open
Portugal	optional referendum	not yet available[3)]	ratified
Romania	parliamentary ratification of the accession treaty	17 May 2005	ratified
Slovakia	parliamentary	11 May 2005	failure
Slovenia	parliamentary	1 February 2005	ratified
Spain	consultative referendum + parliamentary (both chambers)	18 May 2005	ratified
Sweden	parliamentary	not yet available[3)]	ratified
United Kingdom	consultative referendum + parliamentary (both chambers)	not yet available[3)]	open

Source:
http://www.eu-ratifikation.de
(Florian Bischof and Almut Möller, Center for Applied Policy Research)

on the EU Constitution. A distinction is generally made between mandatory referendums, where the result is legally binding, and consultative referendums, where the result is not legally binding.

2) The current state of the ratification process can be seen under www.eu-ratifikation.de.

3) After the failed referendums in France and in the Netherlands ratification has been postponed indefinitely.

it more difficult for member states to form blocking coalitions and promotes the ability to form constructive majorities. Furthermore, the extension of majority decisions in the Council of Ministers is essential for the problem-solving competence of an enlarged EU. Finally, the rights of national parliaments should be enhanced ("early warning mechanism"), elements of direct democracy should be introduced ("citizens' initiative"), and the European Parliament should be given greater budgetary powers and co-decision rights in the legislative process.

(3) Reform and enhancement of the instruments of differentiated integration

In the enlarged EU the interests of the member states are becoming more and more diverse. For this reason, strategies of differentiated integration are particularly important. Blockades or the lack of political will in certain member states in the fields of monetary, internal and social policy were already in the past overcome with the help of differentiation, thereby promoting the process of integration. The amendment of the current Treaties should include the reforms of the existing instruments laid down in the Constitution ("enhanced cooperation") and adopt the new instruments especially in the area of the European Security and Defence Policy.

(4) Other constitutional innovations

Finally, a series of central provisions of the European Constitution should be adopted as part of a reform of the current Treaties. These include the legally binding incorporation of the Charter of Fundamental Rights, the introduction of competence categories, the adoption of the so-called "passerelle" or "bridging clauses," which aim to make it easier to reform the European Treaties, the adoption of the solidarity clause, and the introduction of the mutual defense clause. It is also of fundamental importance to reform the procedure for future revisions of EU primary law. Here the Constitutional Treaty does not go far enough. Ever since the "no" votes in France and the Netherlands it has become evident that the agreed procedure whereby such matters are referred to the European Council is insufficient.

The modesty of a "Treaty Amending the Treaty of Nice" offers a realistic solution for the current constitutional crisis. However, an obvious consequence of any pragmatic approach would be the loss of its important achievement: the gathering of all the Treaties into a single systematically arranged document.

Dissatisfaction with the European project remains most pressing challenge

Whatever happens during the German Presidency in 2007 with respect to the constitutional stalemate, it is clear that the referendum defeats signify a weak point for the future of European integration. Two years after the Constitution was signed, the electorate's dissatisfaction with the European project remains the most pressing challenge facing political leadership. The EU and its member states, more than ever before, need to conduct a dialogue with citizens about what Europe means, what it stands for, what it should do, and how far its geographical borders should expand.

10 Outlook: the Constitution's future

The European Constitution, in the minds of those who drew it up, is designed to make Europe more approachable for EU citizens. They wished to overcome the compromises adopted in Nice and to replace the old Treaties with a document based on a clear and simple structure which, in the words of the President of the Convention, Valéry Giscard d'Estaing, "every normal person can easily read." The current Constitution has not yet reached this goal. However, Parts I, II and IV provide what one would ask from a classical constitution. As Jack Straw, former British Foreign Secretary, said: "Now, set out in part I of the Constitution, is what the EU has needed for years: clarity and coherence about where its powers come from, and how decisions are made. And, at just 59 short articles, this part, which sets the framework for the Union, could easily fit into anyone's pocket."

The Constitution is better than people think

The Treaty could have been better than it is (see table, p. 58). However, in the end, the voters in France and the Netherlands rejected a document that represents aspirations they broadly support: more transparency, more democracy, modified institutions, more grass-roots politics. So one can interpret their "no" vote as an expression of the fact that EU citizens would have liked to have had a greater say in the constitutional process instead of being confronted with a text imposed on them "from above."

The crisis is also an opportunity

Immediately after the French and Dutch "no" votes, Jean-Claude Juncker, the Luxembourg President whose country was presiding over the EU at the time, declared that "Europe is not in crisis, it is in a deep crisis." But the current crisis in the ratification process and the self-administered "period of reflection" also add up to an opportunity, since Europe's citizens will now have to discuss the contents of the Constitution. Politicians will have to try to make the EU seem more acceptable to the electorate, and take account of its wishes and anxieties. There needs to be a public debate, in the course of which even the critics might begin to understand that the Constitutional Treaty, even if it is not perfect, will provide Europe with valuable improvements.

EU citizens ought to be aware of the fact that, in the absence of a Constitution, the Treaty of Nice will continue to remain in force. Decision-making in a European Union with 27 or more will soon become more difficult and protracted. If the Constitution cannot take effect, it will be necessary to consider a kind of treaty amending the Treaty of Nice.

The Constitution provides only the basic rules

However, it also needs to be made clear that the European Constitution can provide no more than a framework. Institutions and decision-making procedures are at the heart of a political system and thus a necessary precondition for political action. Yet, they merely establish the basic rules. Developing specific political ideas on the basis of the Constitution is the task of political decision-makers: the governments of the member states, the members of the European Parliament, the members of the Commission and also the national parliaments.

More and more legislation now comes from Brussels. For this reason, European politics increasingly has a specific influence on the member states' domestic policies. In the final analysis, the ratification process has demonstrated that in the future, EU citizens must have a greater say in European politics.

An opportunity for a fresh start

Europe needs a plan to save not only the constitutional project, but also the future of integration. Politicians need to develop a central idea about the future of Europe that will make the EU more approachable for its citizens. The constitutional crisis in this sense provides us with an opportunity—the chance for a fresh start.

Appendix

The Constitution from A to Z

The ABC of the European Constitution elucidates important elements and concepts of the Treaty establishing a Constitution for Europe, in particular those which are being introduced for the first time.

Bridging clause

The "passerelle" or bridging clause makes it possible for the EU to make decisions without lengthy negotiations at an intergovernmental conference. In Part III of the Constitutional Treaty, areas of unanimity can be transferred to majority decisions and the special legislative procedure to the ordinary legislative procedure (Article IV-444 TCE) on the basis of a unanimous decision of the European Council. By making it more difficult for the member states to exercise the right of veto and by strengthening the European Parliament, it will be possible in the future to improve the EU's ability to act and its democratic legitimation with the help of the bridging clause and without resorting to the complicated treaty revision procedure.

Citizens' initiative

The direct influence of citizens on the policies of the EU is strengthened by the introduction of a "European citizens' initiative." The European Commission must submit legislative proposals for a certain issue if it is asked to do so by at least a million citizens from a "significant" number of member states (Article I-47 TCE).

Co-decision procedure

The co-decision procedure strengthens the European Parliament, which participates in legislation on an equal footing with the Council of Ministers. However, it is not used for all kinds of legislation. Its universal application is the goal of the EU Constitution, which raises the co-decision procedure in conjunction with the double majority in the Council of Ministers to the status of the "ordinary legislative procedure." At the same time, the areas in which the co-decision procedure is used are expanded.

Double majority

The purpose of the double majority is to ensure that an enlarged Union is in a position to take action, and to enhance the democratic legitimacy of the decision-making process. From November 1, 2009, there will be majority decisions in the Council of Ministers in accordance with Article I-25 TCE if 55 percent of the states (at least 15), which at the same time represent 65 percent of the EU population, are in favor of a motion (see the detailed explanations on pp. 77–78). These two criteria are a reflection of the fact that on the one hand the EU is a union of states, and on the other a union of citizens. The double majority replaces the complicated triple majority of the Treaty of Nice. The latter includes also a negotiated number of votes for each member state, which reflects the size of the population (qualified majority).

Early warning system/mechanism

This instrument is designed to enable the parliaments of the member states to appeal at an early stage against Commission proposals whenever they believe that they infringe on the → principle of subsidiarity. Hitherto, the national parliaments have been restricted to the indirect path of participating internally in the European policy of their governments. The Constitutional Treaty now accords them the right to have a direct influence on the decision-making processes, and of lodging an appeal with the European Court of Justice.

Enhanced cooperation

Enhanced cooperation, which was introduced in Amsterdam, and modified in Nice and by the Constitutional Treaty, is the general instrument of differentiated integration. In accordance with Article I-44 TCE, member states, under certain circumstances, can cooperate more closely than the EU level envisages. However, in doing so they must make use of EU institutions and procedures. Enhanced cooperation may be used only in the last resort if the project in question cannot be implemented simultaneously with all the EU states. Enhanced cooperation must serve the basic goals of the Union, be implemented by at least eight EU countries (Nice) or a third of the member states (Constitution), and be open to all the member states. All the members of the Council may take part in the consultations held within the framework of such cooperation. However, when it comes to making decisions, only those countries participating in a specific case of enhanced cooperation are entitled to vote (see also Chapter 8.7).

European Convention

This body was convened in order to reform the European Treaties. What was known as the European Convention had 105 members and their deputies, and comprised government representatives, members of the national parliaments, members of the European Parliament, and members of the EU Commission. Delegates from the accession states also took part in the Convention. It was chaired by the former French President Valéry Giscard d'Estaing. His deputies were former Prime Ministers Giuliano Amato (Italy) and Jean-Luc Dehaene (Belgium).

European Defence Agency (EDA)

The purpose of the newly created agency is to encourage cooperation among the member states in matters relating to armaments and the development of defense and armaments policy in the countries of the EU. Article I-41 TCE states that it is to make a contribution to research and procurement.

European External Action Service

Article III-296 TCE establishes a European External Action Service (EAS). It is made up of officials from the General Secretariat of the Council, the Commission and the member states. The EAS supports the Union Minister for Foreign Affairs and works together closely with the diplomatic services of the member states.

European symbols

European symbols are designed to help people to identify with the EU and to suggest its proximity to EU citizens. They are listed prominently in Article 1-8 TCE:

- the blue flag with a circle of twelve golden stars
- the anthem "Ode to Joy" from Ludwig van Beethoven's Ninth Symphony
- the EU motto, "United in Diversity"
- the euro as the common currency
- Europe Day, which is celebrated throughout the Union on May 9

Intergovernmental conference

Intergovernmental conferences are convened to examine, adapt and amend the European Treaties. Each EU member state sends negotiators to discuss the amendments. Intergovernmental conferences usually last for several months. At the end of the consultations, the Heads of State and Government must adopt the new treaty provisions on the basis of unanimity. The Treaties of Maastricht, Amsterdam and Nice, and also the Treaty establishing a Constitution for Europe are the result of intergovernmental conferences. The new Constitutional Treaty can only enter into force when all the member states have adopted it in accordance with their domestic procedures (parliaments and/or referenda).

Legal personality

The European Union is attributed a single legal personality in the European Constitution. This means that it can sign internationally binding treaties or join international organizations. Hitherto, only the EC (as part of the EU) had a single legal personality, which led to the confusing and simultaneous use of the concepts "EC" and "EU." Thus the single legal personality also makes everything easier to understand. The Constitution simply refers to the "EU."

National parliaments

The Constitution has enhanced the importance of the national parliaments. The → early warning system makes it incumbent on the European Commission to inform the parliaments in good time about proposed legislation. These can then lodge an appeal if they perceive an infringement of the → principle of subsidiarity.

Open methods of coordination

This refers to types of procedure which are intended to help the member states solve problems relating to structural reforms in their own country by "taking a peek over the fence." For this purpose, the Council of Ministers can set out common goals and guidelines, for example, in the fight against poverty and social exclusion. The member states can then decide on which measures they wish to use in order to attain the stated aims. The process is regularly supervised by the Commission and evaluated in order to promote mutual learning. Open methods of coordination are not legally binding.

Permanent structured cooperation

The relevant clause in Article I-41 TCE pertains to the area of European Security and Defence Policy. Member states that wish to participate must not only demonstrate the necessary political will, but also be able to take the kind of military action required. Permanent structured cooperation is initiated by a European decision with qualified majority. The participating countries can assume military responsibilities which go beyond the EU level (see also Chapter 8.7).

Post-Nice process

In the aftermath of the Treaty of Nice there was a public debate about large-scale structural reforms in the EU (greater clarity with regard to the assignment of competences, simplification of the Treaties, incorporation of the Charter of Fundamental Rights, appropriate role for the national parliaments). The post-Nice process led to the → Convention, which drew up the Treaty establishing a Constitution for Europe adopted by the → Intergovernmental Conference.

President of the European Council

The European Council will henceforth be an official EU institution. Hitherto, the chair in the European Council changed twice a year. The Constitutional Treaty seeks to streamline European politics and to give it a human face. In accordance with Article I-22 TCE, a President of the European Council will be elected by the Heads of State and Government with qualified majority for a period of two-and-a-half years. His or her principal tasks are the preparation for and chairing of the meetings of the European Council. He or she represents the interests of the Union externally. Together with the Union Minister for Foreign Affairs and the President of the Commission, he or she is part of the EU's leadership trio.

Qualified majority

Decisions in the Council are made on the basis of unanimity, of a simple majority (i.e., a majority of the votes cast), or of a qualified majority. The qualified majority as specified in the Treaty of Nice currently comprises three preconditions. The majority of member states must be in favor of a motion and at the same time this majority must also comprise 62 percent of the total EU population. On top of this, each member state, depending on its size, has a certain number of votes, of which a certain quorum (a specified number of votes is needed in order to be able to make a decision) must have been reached. From 2009 onwards, the requirements will be simplified, since the vote-based criterion is to be abolished (→ double majority). The Constitutional Treaty has extended the areas in which decisions are made on the basis of a qualified majority.

Reference to God

The reference to God was a controversial issue in the process of drawing up the EU Constitution. The Constitutional Treaty does not contain a direct reference to God, and does not explicitly mention Europe's Christian roots. The Preamble refers to the cultural, religious and humanist inheritance of Europe, from which have developed the universal values of the inviolable and inalienable rights of the human person, freedom, democracy, equality and the rule of law.

Solidarity clause

The solidarity clause in Article I-43 of the Constitutional Treaty states that the Union and its members must act in a spirit of solidarity. This means that, in the event of a terrorist attack or a natural disaster, a member state will be supported by the others with all the resources at their disposal. In the wake of the terrorist attack in Madrid in March 2004, the European Council agreed to the early use of this clause.

Subsidiarity principle

The subsidiarity principle states that decisions should be made on a level that is closest to the citizens. It should always be asked whether joint action is really justified in view of what can be done on the national, regional or local levels. In the areas for which it is not exclusively responsible, the European Union takes action only if what it proposes to do is more effective than national, regional or local measures. Coupled with subsidiarity are the principles of proportionality and necessity. This means that the EU measures may not go beyond what is necessary to achieve the Treaty goals. The EU Constitution introduces a new form of subsidiarity control (→ early warning system/early warning mechanism).

Treaty revision procedure

According to Article IV-443 TCE, proposals for the revision of the EU Constitution may be submitted to the Council of Ministers by any member state, the European Commission or the European Parliament. After consulting the European Parliament and the Commission, the European Council can convene a convention to examine the proposed amendments. An intergovernmental conference then has the final say in the matter. The European Council can also decide not to convene a convention if the amendments do not justify it. In this case, the decision is left to an intergovernmental conference. Amendments to the EU Constitution have to be ratified by all the member states in accordance with their respective constitutional requirements.

Union Minister for Foreign Affairs

This office combines the functions of the Commissioner for Foreign Affairs and the High Representative of the Common Foreign and Security Policy (known as "Mr. or Mrs. CFSP"). The Union Minister for Foreign Affairs is appointed by the European Council with the consent of the President of the Commission. According to Article I-28 TCE, he or she is responsible for the Common Foreign and Security Policy of the European Union, chairs the Foreign Affairs Council, and is at the same time one of the Vice-Presidents of the European Commission.

Withdrawal clause

Hitherto, the EU Treaties did not include provisions allowing a country to withdraw from the EU. The new Constitutional Treaty makes provision for this eventuality in Article I-60 TCE. Each member state can decide to leave the EU. It must notify the European Council of its intention. The European Council will negotiate and conclude an agreement with this state concerning its withdrawal. In addition to the details of the withdrawal, it will be necessary to determine the framework for its future relationship with the EU.

Picture credits

page 9: Ulli Hartmann
pages 12, 16: Andreas Hermann, Stadt Aachen
pages 19, 23, 24, 25, 27, 30, 45: European Community, Audiovisual Service, Brussels

Werner Weidenfeld

Partners at Odds

The Future of Transatlantic Relations—
Options for a New Beginning

2nd edition 2007, 188 pp., paper
€ 24,–
ISBN 978-3-89204-880-0

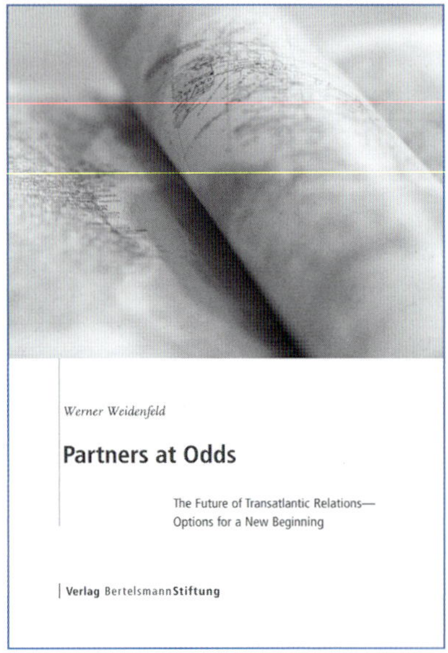

Europe and America are currently experiencing the demise of what had been taken for granted in transatlantic relations for over 50 years. Their relationship has been sucked into the vortex of the global political upheaval that followed the terrorist attacks of 9/11. Europe and America are now faced with the task of finding new answers to the new constellations that have emerged.

Recurring on Europe's and America's common history, Werner Weidenfeld shows the problems and challenges of transatlantic cooperation and outlines possible ways of improving it.

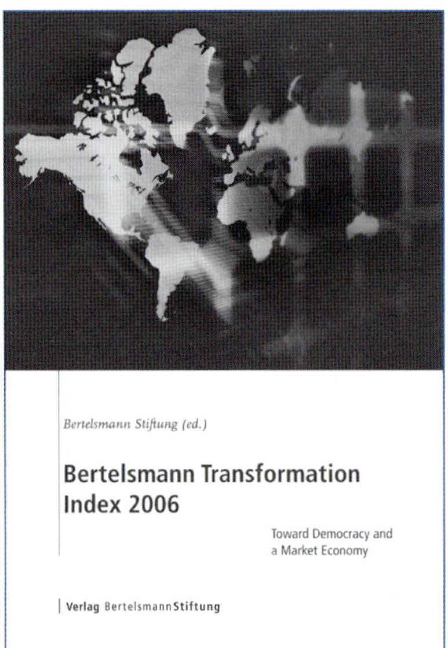

Bertelsmann Stiftung (ed.)

Bertelsmann Transformation Index 2006

Toward Democracy and a Market Economy

2006, 246 pp., paper
incl. CD-ROM
€ 38,–
ISBN 978-3-89204-856-5

Around the world, under widely differing conditions and with varying degrees of success, reform-oriented groups are struggling to democratize their countries and to strengthen the market economy. The peaceful transition from authoritarian regimes poses enormous challenges for citizens and politicians alike.

The Bertelsmann Transformation Index compares the status of democracy and market economy on an international basis (Status Index) and provides comprehensive data on the quality of political management in 119 transition countries from 2003 to 2005 (Management Index).